Vesta in Astrology
Sacred Hearth Within

By Erik M. Roth

Inspiral Nexus Astrology, Inc.
Beaverton, Oregon

Vesta in Astrology ~ Sacred Hearth Within

By Erik M. Roth

Published by
Inspiral Nexus Astrology in association with Goddess Ink

First Edition
Cover and Book Design: Rebekkah Dreskin
Printed in the United States of America
ISBN: 978-1-7333866-7-8

Contents

Acknowledgments

~

There is much that I am grateful for to be identified in this section. First, I am thankful for the privilege of embarking on the journey to become an astrologer via Daniel Giamario and his Shamanic Astrology Paradigm™, which unequivocally changed my life beginning in 2004. I also wish to thank Cayelin Castell, for her inspiration and co-creative efforts with me in the Shamanic Astrology Mystery School and her equally inspiring Venus Alchemy webinar series. Abundant thanks also to Andrea Sansoni and Kate McKee, who helped guide me to shamanic astrology and Daniel.

I am grateful for the contributions and wisdom from author and friend Taylor Ellwood and the friendship of Bruce Hamilton, astrologer Emily Trinkaus, Rowen Foxx, Cynthia Rae, Mary Kern, Felix Warren, Zan Steinberg, and Peter Klein, as well as all those who helped deepen my knowledge of astrology by receiving readings and classes from me.

Thanks also goes to other authors and astrologers whose work influenced me (a partial list but representative): Dane Rudhyar, authors Giorgio de Santillana and Hertha von Dechend of *Hamlet's Mill*, James Hillman, James Hollis, Demetra George, Carlos Castaneda, Emily Trinkaus, Graham Hancock, Joseph Campbell, Sylvia Pererra, Carl Jung, Dan Millman, Paulo Coelho, Bernadette Brady, Robert Graves, Charles Ponce, William Tyler Olcott, Maureen Murdock, Nick Dagan Best, Esther Harding, and author Richard Tarnas of *Cosmos and Psyche.*

I am grateful for the guidance around this book project from Anne Key of Goddess Ink, my editor Barbara Kohl, and cover artist Rebekkah Dreskin, without whom this book would not have come into being so marvelously.

And a special thanks to my eternal love, Gaia and all our relations; the sky of day and night, which has become a temple of sorts for me; the precursor to Saturn, Enki from ancient Mesopotamia and Inanna; the planets, asteroids, and other cosmic guides and teachers. Also, my gratitude flows to all of the ancient skywatchers, priests, priestesses, druids, astrologers, shamans, wiccans, observers, mathematicians, and scientists who tuned in and kept observing and looking up at the sky with open minds, hearts, and soulful longing.

And thank you, Vesta/Hestia, for assisting in teaching us about the sacred.

Preface

‿

Stated most succinctly, my purpose in writing this volume is to open up a deeper understanding of Vesta's contribution to astrology, and more specifically, to the Shamanic Astrology Paradigm™. In early 2013, when I noticed the massive Vesta returning extremely close to its original position in a friend's birth chart on her twenty-ninth birthday, I challenged myself to learn the effects of Vesta's twenty-nine–year cycle and whether other or longer cycles involving Vesta exist. Henceforth, I studied the mysteries of Vesta from a mythological perspective in Demetra George and Douglas Bloch's landmark book, *Asteroid Goddesses*.

Beyond *Asteroid Goddesses*, there was little information in the astrology literature about Vesta. In 2011, NASA's *Dawn* spacecraft began to collect the first close-up photos of this massive asteroid (and later, the dwarf planet, Ceres). In addition, my attention was riveted on certain synchronicities around the resonance of orbits between Saturn and Vesta related to discovering the sacred within us as we mature into adults that are vital to our spiritual growth and knowledge about ourselves and the universe around us.

In my research, I focused on the Vesta/Hestia archetype through works in psychology, mythology, and astrology by Carl Jung, James Hillman, Esther Harding, Robert Graves, Demetra George, and Ginette Paris, among others, as well as understanding Vesta's synodic cycle (the asteroid's relationship to the Sun from the perspective of observing it from Earth). A powerful theme was the concept of sacredness and the asteroid's relationship with the planet Saturn in its orbit. My earliest work on how Vesta and Saturn individually and in relationship to one another impact our lives was presented at the 2013

Shamanic Astrology Conference in Arizona. I then recorded two teleclasses (the first in cooperation with Cayelin Castell) for the Shamanic Astrology Mystery School centered on understanding the role Vesta plays in our lives.[1] The classes can be found on the school's website, shamanicastrology.com. In addition to results of my research and understanding of Vesta's role in astrology and shamanic astrology, I presented selected details about the dwarf planet, Ceres, and the large asteroids, Juno, Pallas Athena, and Hygeia.

This research has also opened up ideas to explore what the role of the dwarf planet Eris has to offer. Another astrologer, Henry Seltzer, wrote a book specifically about Eris called *The Tenth Planet* in 2015, which I found helpful for using Eris in the natal chart and edifying our journeys in life.

My hope for this book is to add to the wealth of astrology texts already available, and that readers will apply this material to their own practice or to indulge their curiosity. I believe these large asteroids add much value to our astrological knowledge and wisdom and will continue to do so in future.

---

1 These classes can be found on the Shamanic Astrology Mystery School's website: shamanicastrology.com.

Introduction

∽

Since humankind's beginnings, we have had a relationship with the sky—the Sun and Moon, the planets, the stars and constellations, and the seasons. The heavens and seasons were perceived as sacred powers in their own right, and thus were beheld with awe and respect. The classic elements of fire, earth, air, and water were also revered and even today are still understood as powerful forces of nature that must be reckoned with. This is what led to the development of astrology.

Although the cosmos or the universe cannot be cognitively defined or understood in totality, we have had many thousands of years to appreciate that life is ever evolving and changing, and its multiple characteristics and dimensions can only be apprehended by the human mind as metaphors working together with emotions and spirit. Hence, the essence or atma of the heavens, the Earth, the elements, and creation itself has been defined by humans as goddesses and gods, heroes, demons, dragons, and centaurs, among countless others.

In the twentieth century, upon our first sighting of the Earth from space, we gained a new sense of reverence for our impeccable planet. The Earth itself, of course, is sacred and in recent decades we have been waking up to the nature of humanity's only home. And while Mother Earth has been revered in many ways by innumerable ancient cultures, the goddess Vesta of ancient Rome (Greek Hestia) specifically symbolized the sacred and revered.

Vesta held communities and homes together around the fire and devoted herself to keeping the flame alive in perpetuity. The fire in the homes and temples was sacred and became a temple unto itself. It was warmth, focus of attention, precious, love, magic, spiritual mystery, and reverence all wrapped into one.

What does it mean to be sacred or hold something as sacred? Is it devotion to something or someone? Is it a kind of passion? Is it related to love? Its origin derives from the Latin words *sacere(s)* and *sacer*, meaning "to make sacred, consecrate, hold sacred, immortalize, dedicate to, hold apart, and to sanctify." From there several words related to sacred were spawned, such as *sacrifice, sacrilege, sacrilegious, sanctum, sacrosanct*, and *sacristy.* "Sacred" feels similar to "holy," but the latter often refers to people and relationships, whereas the former is used for events, objects, and places (natural or otherwise), that is, something related to the divine. The two terms are occasionally used interchangeably. For purposes of this writing, I will use the word *sacred* to refer to that ineffable something we hold true to ourselves and our communities, an inner fire (of varying qualities) that is intended to be held in reverence within even as we express it without, or in the world. While the words *sacred* and *sacredness* have only been with us since their Latin origins, the qualities or meanings of those words, of course, have been expressed among us for as long as humans have recognized mysteries in the world.

What has been deemed *sacred* in the last five thousand years typically pertained to institutionalized religious and/or spiritual traditions across the world. Many things related to sacred mysteries derive from our relationship with the Earth and the cosmos. From this recognition and with it, our feelings of wonder and reverence, came the first of the megalithic structures around the world on nearly every continent. These structures were dedicated to observing the mysteries in the sky and their relationship to us. Temples, stone circles, pyramids, pillars, towers, and other artifacts were living libraries, monuments to the great patterns of our world. The stars, planets, Sun, and Moon lived within us and we saw divinity in all. Nature itself lived within us and we within Nature; there was no distinction or separation of human beings and the world/cosmos around us. We took it in through breath, sustenance, and all that we felt.

The current seasonal or temporal astrology signs (Capricorn, Aries, Gemini, Scorpio, etc.) were not invented until 432 BCE by a man named Euctemon and the earliest recorded personal astrology charts came about around this time. The zodiacal constellations originally bore the same names but due to the Earth's wobble or precession of the equinox, the seasonal points of Earth shift gradually to different parts of the sky. Today, the ancient names of the constellations are still in use. In my own practice and in shamanic astrology, we tend to refer to the zodiacal constellations more directly by what they were known as in ancient times: The Ram, The Bull, The Twins, The Crab, The Lion, The Priestess, The Scales, The Scorpion, The Archer (not a centaur archer), The Goat-Fish, The Water-Bearer, and The Fish.

The constellations, which help inform the seasonal signs and the essence of those signs, are an important part of our relationship with the sky. One of the key tenets in shamanic astrology is about humans developing a relationship with the sky, planets, Moon, Sun, and stars. For most of humanity's history, we were deeply connected to the sky in our daily lives. Archaeologists and anthropologists continue to study and document expressions of human relationships with the cosmos found in sites everywhere in the world. One example of how ancient peoples experienced an intimate relationship with the sky is described in the 2010 documentary film, *Cave of Forgotten Dreams*. One of the paintings from the Chauvet caves in southern France dated over 30,000 years ago depicts The Bull constellation (currently known as the Taurus constellation).[2]

The elements of classic/early times and the heavens presented mysteries that were related to the various pantheons of gods and goddesses and spirits. They do not fit into the periodic

2 For details on the documentary, see en.wikipedia.org/wiki/Cave_of_Forgotten_Dreams.

table of elements or in any type of neat boxes of labels. These mysteries continue to evoke provocative images, emotions, actions, wisdom, and knowledge, which are as symbolically infinite as the actual cosmos. Astrology as a study, philosophy, and language (not "science" in the modern sense) attempts to guide us in understanding these mysteries. In its essence, astrology holds no judgment or bias. It is simply present for all to experience in the heart, body, mind, and soul.

Mythology of Vesta/Hestia

Vesta or Hestia, a goddess of ancient Mediterranean cultures, symbolized the sacred hearth fire in the home and the community. In Roman mythology, Vesta is the third daughter of Saturn, and Juno and Ceres are her sisters. Vesta was equated to the Earth itself, from which fire springs forth. From Greece comes Hestia, the daughter of Cronus (aka Saturn) and Rhea, along with sisters Hera and Demeter. From Ovid's *Fasti*, Vesta is "nothing other than living flame." Hestia, in turn, was the most honored Goddess in households and communities in ancient Greece and surrounding areas. In the Hymn to Aphrodite, Homer wrote, "In all temples of the gods she is honored, and among all mortals she is venerated." For the purposes of this book, I use Vesta and Hestia interchangeably as both contribute to the mysteries of the sacred and the divine nature of the hearth fire.

In *Asteroid Goddesses*, Demetra George and Douglas Bloch describe in detail "the goddess of the hearth fire." Hestia's roots were deep in the pre-Hellenistic Mediterranean world. James Hillman writes in "Hestia's Proposition"[3] that in Latin, the hearth means "*focus*, which can be translated into psychological language as the centering attention that warms to life all that comes within its radius."[4] This is not the same way that Apollo the sun god warms those around him, but rather in a way that provides inner or heart(h) warmth. Her sole purpose

---

3 James Hillman, *Mythical Figures: Uniform Edition of the Writings of James Hillman*, vol. 6 (Putnam, CT: Spring Publications, Inc., 2007), 235.
4 Ibid.

was to care for the sacred flame at the center of the home and community/city.

This fire of mystery, magic, love, and reverence was cared for by Vesta priestesses who in turn were treated as sacred. Fire is a core classical element, alongside earth, water, and air. Humans' great respect for the four elements is old, beyond ancient. Fire was honored by humans for its magical qualities that served to keep predators and insects away (fire and smoke), as well as providing warmth and heat turned to manifold uses. Fire was also recognized for its sacred qualities as it was greatly attractive and even mesmerizing to humans, thereby becoming a gathering place for families, small tribes, villages, and communities. Those who possessed the knowledge to make fire appear when and where they wanted were held in high regard.

Hestia's priestesses in the pre-Hellenistic world of the Mediterranean, the vestal virgins, were sovereign women who bucked the tide of the rising patriarchy, and as Demetra George and Douglas Bloch put it, they were "whole and complete unto themselves...."[5] These priestesses did not commit themselves to marriage or celibacy, instead devoting themselves to the great mother goddess, tending the fires of the hearth, and also voluntarily giving themselves sexually to visitors as part of a sacred rite to the goddess.

The hearth, the focal point of the home, was a symbol of protection or sanctuary, as anyone invited into a home around the hearth was protected from harm perpetrated by others. In *Pagan Meditations: The Worlds of Aphrodite, Artemis and Hestia*, Ginette Paris writes, "Quarrels and fights could not develop in Hestia's presence, because the hearth was a place of peace and security. As Plato remarked, when the Gods quarreled, only Hestia did not take part."[6] The hearth was a place

5 Demetra George and Douglas Bloch, *Asteroid Goddesses* (San Diego, CA: ACS Publications, 1986), 121.
6 Ginette Paris, *Pagan Meditations: The Worlds of Aphrodite, Artemis, and Hestia* (Putnam, CT: Spring Publications, 1986), 168.

of energetic focus that the vast majority of humanity has lost; we grieve, yearn for it in modern times, mostly unconsciously.

In Robert Graves' book, *The White Goddess*,[7] Vesta is connected to the pre-Christian mother goddess Diana as well as Nemesis (from Greek *nemos* or "grove"), another name for the goddess, which in classical Greek also connotes divine vengeance for breaches of taboo. A reference to the sacred and breaking of taboo suggests that in ancient times, breaking from tradition meant disturbing the golden sacred hearth, the woven patterns or tapestry that brought about and sustained harmony among human beings and their environment. The sacred grove was a place of magic and reverence in the ancient world, especially concerning Vesta or Hestia. We can think of this as nature's focus or hearth where people come together under the goddess's protection to conduct ceremony. The groves were sacred places—in short, a natural temple on or within Mother Earth.

As George and Bloch have done in *Asteroid Goddesses*, Robert Graves in *The White Goddess* connected the ancient practices of Hestia priestesses to sacred sexuality, long eradicated by the monotheistic religions and patriarchal cultures of the Western world. The temples of Vesta/Hestia were loaded with phallus symbols. Sacred ceremonies by vestal virgins and the oak king's companions in certain places during the pre-Hellenistic Greek period ensured that future kings were born from the womb of a vestal virgin.[8]

According to George and Bloch, "Each year at midsummer a marriage feast of the oak-queen and oak-king was arranged in which six vestals coupled with six of the oak-king's twelve companions. The promiscuous lovemaking took place in the darkness of a sacred cave so that nobody knew who lay with whom nor who the father was of any child born of such couplings. If

---

7   Robert Graves, *The White Goddess*, amended and enlarged ed. (Toronto: McGraw-Hill Ryerson, 1948; New York: Farrar, Straus and Giroux, 1986), 255.
8   Ibid., 357.

the oak-queen failed to birth a son, the new king was chosen from a child born to a vestal...."[9] Such practices are also embedded in the Virgo astrological archetype, which is rooted in the roles of such revered priestesses over countless millennia.

As an archetype, Vesta/Hestia truly places sacredness and sacred or revered duty above all else. Hestia is generally accepted as a cousin to Vesta during the times of the Roman empire, when temple priestesses/vestal virgins were celibate for specific periods of time. After the empire collapsed, patriarchy continued to transform society—men became dominant and women subordinate, although men often feared women. This fear led to religious doctrines in Europe, North Africa, and Asia that distorted the goddess Hestia/Vesta, where the priestess (nun) not only had to be celibate but also devoted to a single male god, nearly eliminating any sovereignty over her own mind, spirit, and body.

The Fire and Earth of Vesta

The Romans, of course, "borrowed" much of the Greek pantheon of goddesses and gods and re-named them. But not all Roman gods and goddesses came from Greece. According to Georges Dumézil, "The Roman theory of fires ... shows agreements with the [east] Indian theory, which go far beyond what Greece, in its cult of Hestia, can demonstrate as Indo-European survivals." Dumézil then comments on the religious use of fires in Rome and a "third fire" that was specifically deified.[10]

In ancient Rome, the central fire, attributed to Romulus, was never created from another fire in the city or elsewhere. It was created from scratch in a special ceremony. All other fires in the city were born from the central fire. The central fire, the

---

9   George and Bloch, *Asteroid Goddesses*, 121.
10   Georges Dumézil, *Archaic Roman Religion: With an Appendix on the Religion of the Etruscans*, vol. 1, (Baltimore: Johns Hopkins University Press, 1996), 319–20.

"beating heart" of the (eventual) city-state, was what kept Rome alive. The other fires of Rome in many hearths and temples dedicated to deities were more transient and generally served a different purpose even as they were connected to the central fire. Fire itself was truly venerated in Vesta's temple, the only round temple in Rome, compared to other temples or sanctuaries that were specifically aligned with the four (or more) directions or the sky. Because Vesta symbolizes the Earth, her temple was round.

Temple of Vesta, Rome by Andy Hay

The fire at Vesta's temple was the "fire of the master of the house."[11] I understand that the word "house" in this context is the temple and/or Earth. The vestals were caretakers of the fire and the temple; thus the fire was an extension of the Earth. In the classical lexicon, the Earth was feminine in nature and fire masculine, meaning that the feminine birthed the masculine.

---

11 Ibid., 317.

Goddesses, Gods, Archetypes, and Astrology

In the West, Vesta/Hestia was largely replaced by the Judeo-Christian mythos. Nearly all ancient gods and goddesses are still fairly well represented, albeit reinterpreted and renamed as saints, angels, and other mythic figures. Even major pagan holidays such as winter solstice/yule (now, Christmas) were imbued with (mainly) Christian stories and blended into the old stories.

More importantly, the gods and goddesses also stayed alive in another way as archetypes. The word "archetype" is credited to Plato about 2,500 years ago and was revisited by Hermes Tristmegistus in the third-century book, *Corpus Hermeticum*, where he describes God as "archetypal light," essentially intimating that God is the prototype of all light. The word came into modern use in a significant way when Carl Jung began to explore archetypes in his writings. Jung described an archetype as "one of the inherited unconscious patterns that constitutes the fundamental structure of the mind." Archetypes are essentially imprints or templates within all of us on a psychic level.

Photo by Harry Carlton Attwood. Vesta, The Roman goddess of the hearth;
Over the main entrance to the 1930s Courtauld House at Eltham Palace.

The goddesses and gods exhibited human qualities that continue to be injected and projected in everything that we are, that is, our actions and our creations. This includes the celestial bodies we see in the sky. Many of our stories and myths are written in the night sky or day sky. We have built hundreds of structures (and spent countless years building them) over many millennia to understand the complexity of the relationship between Earth and Sky.

Astrology then is a key outcome of humanity's study of the Earth–Sky relationship. Thousands of years ago, astrology was not often used for creating an individual's astrology "chart" or "horoscope." Rather, it was typically used as more of a collective look at humanity's place on Earth and in the cosmos, such as unveiling patterns of the Earth's seasons and how to navigate them. Our ancestors understood the stars, Sun, planets, and Moon as part of a larger pattern that helped us understand change on a collective level and only occasionally on a personal level.

While the goddesses, gods, and spirits (among many other names) became more refined in the Western world at least 6,000 years ago, these deities and other beings have likely been around as long as there have been humans to relate to them. When humans gazed at the cosmos enveloping the Earth, they perceived and felt the presence of these deities. Stories were created based on the cycles and patterns in the sky, and the goddesses and gods played major roles in their movements over time. Over the millennia, these deities involved themselves in the deepest levels of our psyche, the collective unconscious.

As Jung writes, "We can see this most clearly if we look at the heavenly constellations, whose originally chaotic forms were organized through the projection of images. This explains the influence of the stars as asserted by astrologers. These influences are nothing but unconscious, introspective perceptions of the activity of the collective unconscious. Just as the constellation patterns were projected into the heavens, similar figures were projected into legends and fairytales or upon historical persons."[12]

While Joseph Campbell's work concurs and shares Jung's perspective on myth, deities, and heroes, we can further expand on this as humanity's stories are literally written in the stars. In *Hamlet's Mill*, Georgio de Santillana and Hertha von Dechend assert that all of our myths and stories originated in the patterning of the cosmos as seen from Earth. In their book, we see the archetypes play out across time and space in infinite varieties.

TRANSMISSION OF THE SACRED THROUGH DIVINE ORDINARINESS

Maureen Murdock writes of Hestia as the "wise woman within," and how this goddess (feminine energy) can take the form of *divine ordinariness*.[13] In the modern age, the goddess energy has expanded beyond the home and community hearth (as in temple, gathering place) into numerous other places to express its sacred or divine energy in ordinary activities. But there is always a return to the hearth/home (for all people, regardless of gender) to care for it both physically and energetically.

What Murdock means by *divine ordinariness* is "seeing the sacred in each ordinary act." An ordinary act is anything routine, such as scrubbing floors, growing food or going to the grocery store, setting the table, cleaning the hearth, or picking up after one's dog. It is about placing "sacred" in all that is done where routine becomes important. It is an act that nourishes the goddess within and connecting to ourselves as a sacred temple or fire within that temple.

---

12 Carl J. Jung, "The Structure of the Psyche," vol. 8 in *Collected Works* (Princeton, NJ: Princeton University Press, 1960), 152–53.
13 Maureen Murdock, *The Heroine's Journey: Woman's Quest for Wholeness* (Boston: Shambhala Publications, 1990), 139–41.

These modern-day acts, especially in Western civilization, are not seen as heroic or talked about much in most stories told. It is not exciting nor does it draw audiences or capture headlines. Divine ordinariness creates a pathway to ourselves, not for getting attention or displaying heroism (as the patriarchy sees it), but in filling lacunae of great importance in life such that without it the "order of things" would inevitably break down on some level.

Moreover, when we act in tune with this goddess with such acts of ordinariness, we can feel our connection to the Earth element in ourselves and the "spark" that fuels the actions to begin. For example, sweeping the floors of a house or business with a broom energetically extends our focus from our hands holding the broom, through the broomstick to the bristles of the brush and to the floor or ground. The sweeping actions and collection of dust and other materials cleans not only the floor but provides a focus and clarity for the person doing the act.

Divine ordinariness can show up more prominently in times of crisis when the mundane acts of life take on a new level of importance that is typically taken for granted, especially those acts that revolve around cleaning and preventative measures. They can make a difference between life and death in times of disasters, wars, and pandemics.

Placing Vesta in Astrology

VESTA'S RELATIONSHIP WITH SATURN

The asteroid Vesta was not officially recognized by astronomers until 1807, but it is possible that this asteroid was noticed by ancient people long before astronomers began using telescopes. Vesta is the only asteroid that we can see with the naked eye from Earth, but only for a few weeks before, during, and after certain oppositions with the Sun.

At first, Vesta, along with Ceres, Juno, and Pallas Athena were thought to be planets. Due to the relative absence of feminine goddess names in the night sky, the astronomers named them after prominent Roman goddesses. It is interesting to note that Vesta was in the astrological sign of Virgo at the time of its modern-day discovery. This is appropriate, since the goddess Vesta is closely associated with Virgo, the Earth priestess archetypal sign. Many years later the four were re-defined as "asteroids" (also called "minor planets").

Officially designated "4 Vesta" by astronomers (meaning the fourth asteroid discovered), it is the second-most massive asteroid after the dwarf planet Ceres, originally called an asteroid before redefined as a dwarf planet by the International Astronomical Union in 2006.[14] Based on the mean diameter of the asteroid at 525.4 kilometers, Vesta has a circumference of about 1,650 kilometers (1,026 miles). This was confirmed by the Dawn spacecraft in 2011–2012.[15]

---

14 See https://en.wikipedia.org/wiki/Ceres_(dwarf_planet).
15 For more information on Vesta's astronomical characteristics, see https://en.wikipedia.org/wiki/4_Vesta.

Vesta's orbit places the asteroid between the orbits of Mars and Jupiter in the solar system and occupies what astronomers call the asteroid belt (see Fig. 1). Vesta (as an asteroid) is the newest planetary object to be merged into shamanic astrology since Chiron was brought into the Shamanic Astrology Paradigm™ in the early 2000s. I brought Vesta forward into shamanic astrology in 2013 after noticing that this asteroid appeared to return to its natal position near the time of my clients' Saturn returns (ages 29–30 and 58–59).

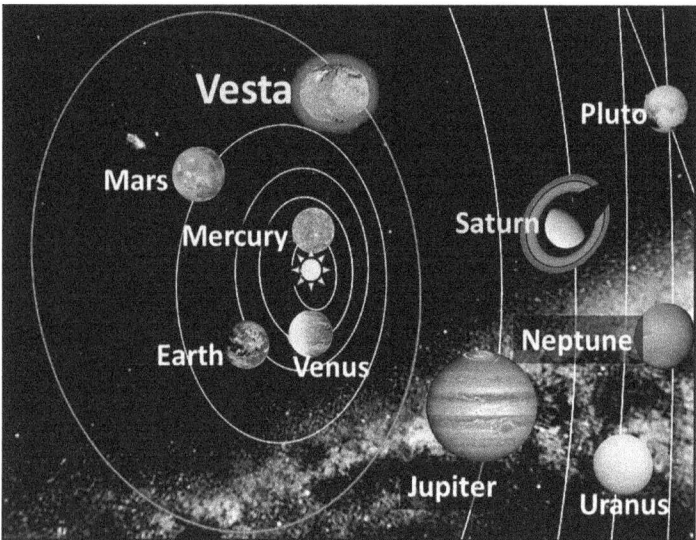

Fig. 1. Vesta's orbit

- Vesta has an "average" orbit of 3.63 years
- Vesta becomes visible (under dark sky conditions) for a short time during the opposition to the sun
- Two full Vesta orbits equal one quarter of a Saturn orbit
- Eight orbits of Vesta (29 years) equals roughly 1 full orbit of Saturn

As a paradigm, shamanic astrology is less complex and technical than other schools of astrology, including traditional Western astrology. Shamanic astrology is a revolutionary paradigm developed by Daniel Giamario. (See Appendix for description of the paradigm.) Practitioners do not typically consider asteroids when devising and weighing meanings found in an astrology chart because important influences were already apparent in the stories of the archetypes (signs), houses, planets, and constellations. But I have learned when studying Vesta's orbital pattern, the knowledge brought forth adds value to the aforementioned Saturn returns, mid-life crises, and other important periods in a person's lifetime. What does Vesta add to the natal chart? In order to answer that question, I begin with Saturn.

At the age of 29–30, the Saturn return is perhaps *the* most powerful initiation during a person's lifetime. Saturn completes one orbit of the Sun, on average, every 29½ years. Saturn, as a planetary initiator, assists people in taking responsibility for their path and being diligent about what they really want here in the 3D world. Saturn represents "reality" and growth through overcoming obstacles and barriers. It sets up a time of great maturation in a human being and coming of age as an adult, especially in terms of responsibilities, commitments, and awareness of what we need to walk our life path.

With respect to commitments to a job/career/vocation, relationships/family, contracts, financial matters—anything to do with "structure" or "bones" of the life span—Saturn is right there to help. Sometimes it may not feel like assistance because of what we think we want versus our soul's path. We may resist the pull to make hard decisions—do the right thing in life—and thereby assign hardship to Saturn. However, a Saturn initiation is not intended to make life difficult. Its process identifies the areas in our lives that need work or those that no longer work for us. Symbolically, we shed our skin during Saturn initiations.

At age 58 to 60 (which varies a little depending on when the person is born in Saturn's orbit relative to Earth), we experience a deeper octave and initiation of the first Saturn return at 29–30. This second Saturn return takes us to the third major phase in the life timeline. Because the average human lifespan is longer now than during the sixteenth century through the mid- to late-twentieth century, we have significant opportunities to take greater responsibility for our life, especially if we had an unfulfilling career or job or have ended a major project, relationship, or significant obligation. When our kids are grown and established in their lives, we are likely considering investment in ourselves in ways that align with our personal truth. Is it time to give back to the community? Is it time to finally take advantage of that calling, vocation, or passion we've thought about for years? What kind of life do we wish to create for ourselves over the next few decades? How do we want to live? These are some of the vital questions that many of us ask ourselves in our late fifties.

The asteroid Vesta adds a valuable element to Saturn initiations, and ultimately, our soul's journey. In shamanic astrology, Vesta in a person's natal chart becomes "sacred devotion to one's inner hearth." There are, of course, twelve versions of that sacred devotion, corresponding to the twelve signs or archetypes in astrology. So, for example, for people born when Vesta was in the sign of Taurus, its influence would be something akin to "sacred devotion to Taurus as their inner hearth," or put another way, "sacred devotion to the art of intimacy or pleasure as their inner hearth." With Vesta, the particular archetype becomes our sacred grove and our way to connect with the Earth.

Vesta exerts a highly personal influence on us that shows up slowly over a lifetime, and it is this archetypal energy (dependent on the sign that Vesta was in at birth) that becomes more "consecrated" within ourselves and how we want to express and/or connect with it. An example of how this archetypal energy manifests can be seen in a client I worked with in the early days of studying Vesta. She was born with Vesta in Gemini. Now, while the astrological house (and any outer planetary aspects) are also important here, let's keep it simple.

This was an area of her chart that stood out because it granted her permission to tap into the sacred clown archetype emerging within—most of the rest of her chart displayed an abundance of service energy, underworld-ness, and seriousness. Gemini has a purpose as an archetype, but it is not bound by rules or laws as are the other signs; thus Vesta in this sign allows for an expression that it is okay to have fun for the sheer sake of doing so.

Another example is a client, Deanna, with Vesta in the sign/archetype of Libra at birth. Libra as an archetype is primarily focused on non-hierarchical, conscious, equal partnership. In her life she has found great rewards and strong motivation upon taking a sacred and ceremonial approach to being in conscious, equal relationships with strong communication as an emphasis. In that kind of relationship, she is honoring her sacred inner hearth of Vesta in Libra.

In my own life, Vesta is expressed through the sign of Aquarius, an archetype only minimally seen elsewhere in my chart. Uranus is a planet that in shamanic astrology has a an astrological resonant energy with the sign of Aquarius when this planet aspects a personal planet/asteroid, like Vesta or an angle of a natal chart (Ascendant/Descendant or Midheaven/Home and Roots). Uranus squares my natal Ascendant/Descendant axis and this adds Aquarius-like qualities to the axis. Compared to the majority of what my chart signifies, archetypally, there are large doses of selfless-service motivations, empathic nature, truth-seeking, and road-tripping (with the combination of Pisces and Sagittarius in my chart). Aquarius, as a sign, is about higher or cosmic consciousness, freedom of mind, unconventionality, eccentricity, rebelliousness, experimentation, detachment, and perceiving higher or universal love and revolutionary motivations. This has certainly shown up in many parts of my life. I do indeed hold those qualities as sacred within, and have worked behind the scenes to incorporate them into my life where it eventually is expressed outside my private life. It became a decidedly spiritual experience to live those described Aquarian qualities.

Bringing Vesta into the Saturn initiation adds a sacred process dimension to the more mundane real-world Saturn initiation, bringing part of the responsibility of one's path to the archetype represented by Vesta in the astrology chart. Our inner hearth is being greatly supported at times when Saturn returns (especially at age 29–30) because Vesta also returns at nearly the exact place when the person was born. Vesta becomes our emphasis during such a time to break new ground tending to the sacred archetypal flame glowing within our soul's field desiring to be noticed and utilized. In short, we experience a Vesta return that overlaps part or the entire period of a Saturn return. The Vesta return adds a deeper dimension to the Saturn return that touches us more subtly than Saturn and focuses on the stewardship of a particular archetype. Mythologically, we can see how Vesta/Hestia would indeed have a powerful relationship with Saturn/Cronos, as this goddess is the daughter of the Titan Saturn/Cronos.

While little as been written elsewhere about the asteroid Vesta in astrology, I fully recommend reading George and Bloch's book, *Asteroid Goddesses*, which covers nearly all of the major asteroids. I was greatly inspired by her research of Vesta; while I do not agree with all of their interpretations of Vesta in astrology, they leave open questions of the various kinds of ways Vesta can express itself in a natal chart. Although I grasp and respect where the authors are coming from in their interpretations, they operate from a different type of Western astrology (what might be called "mainstream" astrology).

In my own experiences with Vesta and having been trained at the Shamanic Astrology Mystery School, I find that Vesta fits quite well into into Giamario's Shamanic Astrology Paradigm™. However, it is more than likely that understanding of the nature of Vesta in astrology will evolve as my experience with it grows.

Erik M. Roth

Placement in the Shamanic Astrology Script

In shamanic astrology, the astrology chart (i.e., natal chart) is perceived as a "map" or "script" of our life purpose and helps us understand the "intent" of each planet's archetypal expression. In the Shamanic Astrology Paradigm™, a natal chart shows us a two-dimensional snapshot of the four-dimensional solar system. The Moon shows us our "lineage" from an archetypal perspective: our past, past-life themes, family, DNA, comfort zones, and addictions. It is also our foundation and typically is something most people identify with, depending on the sign/archetype the Moon happens to be in when a person is born.

The script consists of three distinct aspects, or movements, as in a symphony—thesis (first movement), antithesis (second movement), new synthesis (third movement). The thesis deals with past-life themes, or original identity. The antithesis, or counterpoint, deals with the tools, equipment, and strategy for the current life. The synthesis comprises the current-life purpose or personal medicine wheel.

The second major part of the script, known as the "tools and equipment," is where our emerging masculine (Mars), feminine (Venus), and mind (Mercury) are found. It also shows us the season we were born into vis-a-vis the Sun's position. In sum, the Sun sign represents the archetypal fuel we "burn" in our lives to assist us in realizing our life purpose.

Vesta's position in the solar system (orbiting between Mars and Jupiter) combined with its archetypal expression showing up later in life places it in the "tools and equipment" area in shamanic astrology. It also acts as a connector between a person's Sun, Mercury, Mars, and Venus archetypes to the synthesis, the third and last section or movement of the script.

The synthesis includes Jupiter and its "path of enlightenment" or "vision quest path"; the Midheaven and our archetypal calling or vocation expressed in the world; and the Ascendant, our emerging personal identity project. This third movement

25

represents the leading edge of our life purpose. Essentially, I look at the Ascendant as the "dawning of our selves" as the soul evolves/involves itself into a new lifetime at birth. The Ascendant is the specific sign (not to be confused with the constellation) that is rising on the eastern horizon (while its polar opposite, the Descendant, our archetypal partnership/relationship intent, is the sign setting on the western horizon. Together the Ascendant and Descendant represent a person's "relationship axis."[16] Basic features of the script are summarized in *Table 1*.

Table 1: Shamanic Astrology "Script" for Natal Chart

Thesis—Lineage	Antithesis—Tools	Synthesis—New
Moon	**Sun**	**Angles of chart**
Represents the lineage—Past-life themes, family history, genetic encoding, and the tribe you come from. Training you have already taken; what you mastered coming into this lifetime.	The fuel we burn to reach life purpose. Not archetype-specific unless conjunct Venus or Mars (only two fifths of people resemble their "Sun sign" descriptions).	*Ascendant* (ASC or AS) The personal identity project. *Descendant* (DSC or DS) The partnership project.
	Vesta Sacred qualities, interests, and duties to emerging self; sacred devotion/inner hearth.	*Midheaven* (MC) The right livelihood project. *Bottom of Chart* (IC) The home and roots project.

16 For full details about the script in shamanic astrology, see Daniel Giamario, with Cayelin Castell, *The Shamanic Astrology Handbook*, rev., exp. 4th ed. (Beaverton, OR: Shamanic Astrology Mystery School, Inc., 2018).

House position of South Lunar Node indicates job you had in your tribe, or specialty you had in your previous training.	Venus Principal archetype of the feminine. In a woman's chart, specific feminine imagery for current life. Emerging goddess. In a man's chart, represents the anima or magical feminine, that is, union with one's inner partner.	House position of North Lunar Node further clarifies life purpose projects. Used in combination with any of four angles, it helps determine your new job in your new tribe or your new specialty in your new training.
Planets near South Lunar Node represent specific skill from previous training.	Mars Principal archetype of masculine. In a man's chart, specific masculine imagery for current life. Emerging god. In a woman's chart, represents the animus or inner masculine, that is, union with one's inner partner.	Jupiter Fastest path or kinds of activities for reaching current life goals quickly. Personal path of enlightenment Planet of vision quest
	Mercury In current life mental cognitive thinking capacities. Emerging perception and communication style.	

Outer planet strategy applies to all three movements.

Saturn—Boundaries and limiting conditions. Structure and form. Our relationship with 3D reality and what works and does not work.

Uranus—Shifting of assemblage point. Events of extreme novelty that bring on dramatic change, unplanned, unexpected, uncontrollable events taking us in new directions.

Neptune—Dreams, visions, new awareness through identity crisis, insights through intuition.

Pluto—Descent into underworld, incorporation of the "shadow," facing deepest fears, and events producing chaos for purpose of empowerment.

Chiron—Fracture point, where deepest wounds are. Wounds must be healed as they become the medicine we carry.

For more information on shamanic astrology, see the Appendix.

Vesta's Movement and Return Cycles

The only asteroid we can see with the naked eye, Vesta was "discovered" in 1807. At that time, the asteroid was located in the sign of Virgo (not the constellation that astronomers call by the same name). Because the asteroid Ceres was reclassified as a dwarf planet in 2006, Vesta is now technically the most massive asteroid. After the recent visit by NASA's Dawn spacecraft, scientists learned that Vesta has many characteristics of a planet, including a core, mantle, and crust.[17]

Astrology is typically dismissed as not relevant by astronomers because it is not "scientific" (at least in terms of how science has been defined in the modern age). Such dismissal ignores the fact that human beings have been in relationship with the sky, the cosmos, for countless millennia, as expressed in the relatively modern disciplines of theosophy, archeo-astronomy, philosophy, and psychology.

---

17   Details can be found at http://science.nasa.gov/science-news/science-at-nasa/2011/29mar_vesta/.

In brief, everyone has a relationship with the Sun, Moon, and planets in our solar system and constellations, whether conscious of the same or not. In the current age, many of us have become too rigid and finite in our understanding of life purpose. One of the profound reasons that astrology has survived for so long is its deep imprinting into our psyche from the countless millennia that humankind has been in relationship with the stars. How we integrate this *understanding* is literally carried within the word: we stand under the stars. We look up for knowledge, answers, and guidance. While such gazing or awareness is hardly where we obtain all guidance, it is deeply natural for us to connect to it consciously.

Vesta's light returns to us on a personal and collective level regularly when it may be visible at opposition with the Sun. (Vesta becoming visible does not occur at every opposition as it varies due to proximity with Earth and Sun in its orbit.) The return of Vesta's light, visible or otherwise, influences our lives, albeit it is not as apparent as, for example, Jupiter or Saturn. However, it is important for our overall life journey.

In the previous section on Vesta's relationship with Saturn, I described how we experience a Vesta return around the time of a Saturn return, which means the asteroid's movement has a close connection to the movement of Saturn across the night sky. It takes Vesta 3.6 years to orbit the Sun and two of those orbits are equal to a one-quarter turn of Saturn around the sky, four orbits to equal one-half of a Saturn orbit, and eight orbits of Vesta to equal a full orbit of Saturn in the sky and the astrology chart (natal chart). Hence the two come together often, especially during the first two Saturn returns in a person's life at 29–30 and 58–59 years of age. Because of eccentricities in Vesta's orbit, it can also return at ages 11, 18, 40, 51, 69, 80, and 87 (before the third Saturn return) as well, but Vesta will not be as close to the natal Vesta position as occurs at age 29 and 58. The "most exact" Vesta return occurs at age 29.

Like all planetary bodies, Vesta has a rhythm and language all its own with connections to the sacred fire that burns within each of us. Vesta's orbit is such that it commonly returns on a person's birthday at ages 11, 18, 29, 40, 51, 58, 69, 80, and 87. In this sequence, time between returns is 7 or 11 years, with the closest returns to the natal position at 29-year intervals[18] (29, 58, and 87). Some of the Vesta-return ages correspond to cycles in the shamanic astrology timeline, such as major Saturn returns, mid-life cycles, and the first nodal return (at age 18-½ to 19). Vesta's role at those times assists a person in unearthing emerging qualities that need to be nurtured and held sacred within the heart.

These returns of the planetoid Vesta allow for a person to realize the *sacred* within themselves, the organic patterning that is vital for long-term health. Vesta is a feminine-energy archetype, but it resides in all genders (as would Jupiter, Moon, or Sun) in shamanic astrology.

An example of how Vesta affects the individual early in life comes from my own experience. When I turned 18, Vesta was just passing into (ingressing into) the sign of Aquarius. Some months after my eighteenth birthday and during this Vesta return cycle (and during the Lunar Nodal return), I experienced my first real connection with the stars. I perceived the entire field of stars for the first time in my life (I grew up in Los Angeles), and it had an enormous impact in my life. I finally saw the immensity of our place in the universe, gaining a certain cosmic awareness and patterning. It was a new feeling of being at home with the celestial realm. (Note: Vesta's natal placement is only 5 degrees from my North Node in the sign of Aquarius.)

The tables created by Rique Pottenger and colleagues in *The Asteroid Ephemeris 1900–2050* are quite helpful for understanding your natal Vesta sign by looking up your birth date.

---

18   Note that 7, 11, and 29 are prime numbers in mathematics.

You can also identify your Vesta sign[19] using astrology software apps available for phones, tablets, and desktop or laptop computers. I primarily use Solar Fire Gold as well as Time Passages.

How does one know the timeframe of a Vesta synodic return? Synodic cycles refer to a planet or other celestial object's meeting with the Sun; the term "synodic" derives from "synod," meaning a meeting place. Thus, Vesta's synodic return begins and ends when it is in opposition to the Sun,[20] and this happens every 24 to 26 months. If you are soon turning age 11, 18, 29, 40, 51, 58, 69, 80, or 87, then you are experiencing a Vesta return. Some Vesta returns may not fall as close to the natal Vesta position as at ages 29, 58, or 87, so their impact as a cycle around the other six birthdays is not as potent but still worth noting.

Regular Vesta synodic cycle

- The synodic cycle of Vesta begins at opposition to the Sun (acronychal rise).
- Start and endpoints of Vesta's synodic cycle occur when the asteroid is visible to the naked eye.
- The cycle can last from about 16 to 17.5 months.
- After 21 synodic cycles of Vesta, it comes very close to exactly 29 years (within 3 to 7 days).

Vesta return cycles

- A Vesta return is as long as its synodic cycle of 16 to 17½ months (Vesta–Sun opposition to Vesta–Sun opposition, if one of a person's birthdays at 11, 18, 29, 40, 47, 51, 69, 80, and 87 falls within that cycle boundary).

---

19 An online example for asteroids is http://www.true-node.com/eph3/#names.
20 This synodic return is similar to Mars, whose synodic cycle begins at the Mars–Sun opposition and ends at the next Mars–Sun opposition while Mars is at its closest and brightest point in the sky. See https://www.inspiralnexus.com/2016/05/your-call-to-adventure for more information.

- A Vesta return takes place when Vesta comes close to its original position during a person's birthday (exceptions occur for those born with Vesta retrograde).
- Vesta returns take place prior to or during the three Saturn returns at 29–30, 58, and 87–88.
- There are other times when Vesta returns (minor) happen, but not as close to natal chart position as occurs at ages 11, 18, 40, 47, 51, 69, and 80. (At 11 and 18 years, the return takes place near the Jupiter and lunar node returns, respectively.)
- With each synodic cycle, there is an "overtone" or the sign in which an acronychal rise occurs.

Vesta's larger "precess" cycles

Every 29 years, Vesta returns nearly exactly to the same place in the sky with a minor difference each time. But over many decades and even a few centuries, that slight difference becomes pronounced. Thus, over five or more periods, the "sign" of the return will "precess" (i.e., move backwards from its apparent position of the original start date) into a new sign, on average.

- Twenty-nine years equates to 21 synodic cycles of Vesta (16 to 17.5 months each).
- Vesta takes an average of 203 years (or seven periods of 29 years) to *precess* from one sign to another (from 145 years to 261 years) at the acronychal rise of Vesta.
- The 29-year Vesta cycle shifts by 3 to 6 degrees in the overtone sign (lower degrees generate longer "precess cycles").
- Saturn's position typically falls within 5–6 degrees every 29 years of Vesta's 21 synodic cycle calibration (which is the 29-year Vesta synodic return).

Vesta's acronychal rise

Astronomically, an opposition between two celestial bodies with the rise of one in the east called an *acronychal rise.* Vesta's acronychal cycle begins when the asteroid becomes visible with the naked eye, requiring 16 to 17-½ months for Vesta to move from one opposition to the next. In shamanic astrology, the acronychal rise point is utilized as the start point (and the end point) of any Mars and Vesta synodic cycle.

The sign of each acronychal rise of Vesta sets the "archetypal overtone" of the entire cycle and further clarifies the expression of Vesta in addition to the sign and the house position of Vesta in the natal chart. This overtone is important first and foremost in helping a person to recognize when their major Vesta returns are taking place (taking into account the precessing of Vesta after each 29-year return, which means returning a small number of degrees earlier than the previous acronychal rise 29 years ago). Second, it adds a small, but important, indefinable amount of the sign of the archetypal overtone to the Vesta natal sign. The extent of the archetypal overtone's influence may be greater in some cases than others. I have found it difficult to quantify how much influence that a city or community has on a person when compared to their parents. This is not a precise analogy but rather a rough comparison.

In the following example of finding a person's Vesta archetypal overtone, I use the information on overtones in 1920 through 2030 at acronychal rise in Table 2. My birthdate, November 25, 1971, falls between the acronychal rise dates of Vesta on July 22, 1971 and November 30, 1972. I then use the acronychal rise date that is closest, but precedes my birthday. Thus, I have a Vesta overtone of Capricorn. The influence of this overtone relates to my treatment of knowledge and systemic patterns through a lens imbued with love and sacredness, especially when I feel they are revolutionary and thus will contribute to humanity's ascension in time.

Table 2: Vesta Archetypal Overtones
in 1920–2030 at Acronychal Rise

Date	Vesta	Saturn
Jun 17 1920	26°25' Sag	6 Vir
Nov 9 1921	17°22' Tau	3 Lib
Mar 3 1923	12°14' Vir	19 Lib
Aug 20 1924	27°36' Aqu	27 Lib
Dec 19 1925	27°25' Gem	21 Sco
May 1 1927	10°32' Sco	6 Sag
Oct 10 1928	17°24' Ari	14 Sag
Jan 29 1930	08°54' Leo	7 Cap
Jul 8 1931	15°40' Cap	20 Cap
Nov 21 1932	29°47' Tau	0 Aqu
Mar 19 1934	28°12' Vir	23 Aqu
Sep 7 1935	13°46' Pis	6 Pis
Dec 31 1936	09°39' Can	17 Pis
May 21 1938	29°55' Sco	14 Ar
Oct 24 1939	00°56' Tau	27 Ar
Feb 11 1941	22°33' Leo	9 Tau
Jul 28 1942	04°51' Aqu	9 Gem
Dec 4 1943	11°57' Gem	24 Gem
Apr 5 1945	15°45' Lib	4 Can
Sep 22 1946	29°17' Pis	6 Leo
Jan 13 1948	22°11' Can	21 Leo
Jun 11 1949	20°24' Sag	1 Vir
Nov 6 1950	13°59' Tau	29 Vir
Feb 26 1952	07°37' Vir	14 Lib
Aug 15 1953	23°05' Aqu	22 Lib
Dec 16 1954	24°10' Gem	17 Sco
Apr 24 1956	04°55' Sco	1 Sag

Table 2: Vesta Archetypal Overtones
in 1920–2030 at Acronychal Rise

Date	Vesta	Saturn
Oct 6 1957	13°46' Ari	10 Sag
Jan 25 1959	05°21' Leo	2 Cap
Jul 2 1960	10°41' Cap	15 Cap
Nov 18 1961	26°29' Tau	25 Cap
Mar 14 1963	23°53' Vir	18 Aqu
Sep 1 1964	09°34' Pis	1 Pis
Dec 28 1965	06°26' Can	12 Pis
May 15 1967	24°19' Sco	8 Ar
Oct 20 1968	27°22' Ari	21 Ar
Feb 7 1970	19°00' Leo	3 Tau
Jul 22 1971	29°28' Cap	4 Gem
Nov 30 1972	08°42' Gem	18Gem
Mar 31 1974	10°47' Lib	29Gem
Sep 18 1975	24°52' Pis	0 Leo
Jan 8 1977	18°42' Can	15 Leo
Jun 4 1978	13°59' Sag	25 Leo
Nov 3 1979	10°29' Tau	23 Vir
Feb 21 1981	03°13' Vir	9 Lib
Aug 10 1982	17°30' Aqu	17 Lib
Dec 13 1983	20°49' Gem	12 Sco
Apr 18 1985	28°45' Lib	27 Sco
Oct 2 1986	09°44' Ari	6 Sag
Jan 21 1988	01°25' Leo	28 Sag
Jun 25 1989	04°31' Cap	11 Cap
Nov 15 1990	23°10' Tau	21 Cap
Mar 8 1992	18°51' Vir	14 Aq
Aug 27 1993	04°51' Pis	26 Aqu

Table 2: Vesta Archetypal Overtones
in 1920–2030 at Acronychal Rise

Date	Vesta	Saturn
Dec 24 1994	03°02' Can	7 Pis
May 8 1996	18°30' Sco	3 Ar
Oct 16 1997	23°50' Ari	16 Ar
Feb 3 1999	15°02' Leo	28 Ar
Jul 16 2000	24°29' Cap	28 Tau
Nov 27 2001	05°30' Gem	12 Gem
Mar 26 2003	05°52' Lib	23 Gem
Sep 12 2004	20°49' Pis	24 Can
Jan 5 2006	15°28' Can	9 Leo
May 30 2007	08°48' Sag	19 Leo
Oct 29 2008	07°00' Tau	18 Vir
Feb 17 2010	29°27' Leo	3 Lib
Aug 5 2011	12°40' Aqu	13 Lib
Dec 9 2012	17°39' Gem	7 Sco
Apr 13 2014	23°28' Lib	22 Sco
Sep 28 2015	05°40' Ari	1 Sag
Jan 17 2017	28°06' Can	23 Sag
Jun 19 2018	28°29' Sag	28 Sag
Nov 12 2019	19°40' Tau	16 Cap
Mar 4 2021	14°23' Vir	9 Aqu
Aug 22 2022	29°39' Aqu	21 Aqu
Dec 21 2023	29°38' Gem	2 Pis
May 1 2025	12°06' Sco	28 Pis
Oct 12 2026	19°56' Ari	11 Ari
Jan 31 2028	11°05' Leo	22 Ari
Jul 9 2029	18°10' Cap	22 Tau
Nov 24 2030	02°07 Gem	6 Gem

* Table was created by author using data from Solar Fire software.
Notes: The acronychal rise of Vesta begins when the asteroid is rising in east and the Sun is setting in the west.

The Twelve Tribes of Vesta

There are twelve major expressions of the asteroid Vesta, archetypally speaking, as there are for each planet, other asteroids, Sun, Moon, and other points in natal chart. Each of the archetypes (astrology signs) has a unique role on life's stage and has been around since humanity's beginnings.

In shamanic astrology, the asteroid Vesta expresses itself through the archetype (as well as the astrological house). You can think of Vesta as the heart rhythm or the pulse of matter within self. My view of Vesta resembling a rhythm or pulse is grounded in the importance of the hearth or sacred center of the home within the human being. The hearth fire's regular rhythm must be maintained, nourished, and treated with reverence for the gifts it provides, including the feeling of being grounded in a personal sanctuary. Hestia/Vesta gave mortals and immortals alike a place in space to feel that rhythm of the home, community, and self. It can be summarized as sacred province, reverence, or devotion to one of the twelve signs.

As mentioned in the previous section, the Sun represents the "fuel we burn"; Mars and Venus are the masculine and feminine principles, respectively; the Moon, one's "lineage"; and the Ascendant one's emerging identity. Vesta's influence is more noticeable when its archetype in the natal chart differs from one's Moon, Sun, Venus, Mars, and/or Ascendant sign. An example would be a person with Vesta in Taurus; the rest of their personal planets are in Leo (Moon), Gemini (Sun), Cancer (Venus), and Virgo (Ascendant). Hence, Vesta's archetype Taurus in this natal chart would stand out more readily.

Vesta, like the planets, Sun, and Moon, has a direct general association with an archetype. For example, Venus has a general association with the sign of Taurus and Mercury with Gemini. For Vesta, that association is with the archetype/sign of Virgo. It means that everyone to varying degrees has Virgo in their chart through the placement of Vesta. This is why I use the word "sacred" in any major description of the sign that Vesta inhabits in a person's chart.

Vesta in Capricorn—Sacred Devotion/Reverence of Ancient Wisdom, Creating the New Operating Manual and Planting the Seeds for the Next Seven Generations

The Capricorn archetype is practical, earthy, and result driven, being devoted contributing to future generations through the knowledge of system structures and creating and maintaining long-lasting structures. This archetype's image, like all archetypes, cannot be finitely defined. However, an image of a teacher loving the role of sharing knowledge and wisdom for present and future generations embodies this sign like no other. Capricorn is a deep earth-element sign and we find that such knowledge is truly stored in the Earth in a physical way revealed by archaeologists, anthropologists, and others who study ancient cultures—the ancients' temples, libraries, and megalithic structures devoted to the Earth and Sky and our relationship with them are found all over the planet.

With Vesta in Capricorn, such knowledge becomes protected as a sacred trust for humanity. Historical examples of the work of Capricorn would be the Great Pyramids of Egypt, the ancient Library of Alexandria, and numerous pyramids in Mesoamerica (Mayan, Toltec, Olmec, etc.) and South America (Inca, pre-Inca cultures) built centuries before the European conquest. Megalithic sites all over Europe such as stone circles are a variety of the sacred trust and certainly connected deeply with the sign/archetype of Virgo and the lineage of priest/ priestesses for millennia.

In modern times, this translates into creating harmony-creating and -sustaining systems that serve humanity and the Earth, such as education, economic, infrastructure, health care and disease prevention systems. Managers, teachers, ministers, directors, and administrators, among others, comprise roles that Capricorn plays in current societies.

When a person has Vesta in Capricorn, it is about creating your own sacred personal systems that serve in the long term but also discovering or formulating systems in society that are in alignment with the greater collective in the long term and holding them in sacred trust. A great example of this is the mythological figure from ancient Mesopotamia, Enki/Ea, who walked the Earth during the golden age of humanity bringing knowledge about agriculture, mathematics, architecture, astronomy/astrology, economics, and law.

Vesta in Aquarius—Sacred Devotion/Reverence for Cosmic Awareness and That Change/ Revolution Is Necessary for Life Evolution

The Aquarius archetype, the revolutionary thinker, comes after Capricornian structures and systems. The role of Aquarius is to evoke novelty, unorthodoxy, and revolutionary ideas to assist humanity in moving beyond stagnant philosophies, systems, structures, religions, and governments that no longer work or serve the greater collective.

Breaking apart and inventing the "new" is a big part of the Aquarian archetypal message. In today's world, that typically involves innovative technologies. In ancient times, Aquarius can be seen as a combination of Prometheus and the Sky God/ Goddess of numerous cultures throughout the globe.

When a person has Vesta in Aquarius, it connects the sacred earth to novel, unorthodox ways of doing things. An

Aquarius Vesta holds and thus brings that which is sacred beyond the limits of systems and structures and into thought experiments and ideas, perhaps implemented in unique ways. It is a mentally creative intellectual sign that can thrive on futuristic change and revolutionary ideas.

Prometheus was the fire-bringer Titan, asked by Athena to bring celestial knowledge to humanity. While Prometheus was punished by Zeus, a patriarchal god, the knowledge nonetheless stayed with humanity. Such wisdom incorporates the exercise of free will and freedom of spirit that we all possess—we can choose to break the chains of our own self-created constraints or structures. Aquarius shows up to share this knowledge with us, which is held in sacred trust across the globe.

Vesta in Pisces—Sacred Devotion/Reverence for Empathy, Creating Safe Space and Merging with Spirit

Pisces is known as the empath or healer archetype in the zodiac. Having Vesta in the sign of Pisces creates a spot for the fire to burn bright for sacred empathy and healing. Pisces as an archetype is devoted to selfless service to others and the divine through the feeling function. It is not an intellectual process, but a process that comes from the heart and soul.

Pisces is also known as the "merge master," which means that Pisces generally desires to merge with others and the divine/spirit. Pisces' empathic nature *feels* for others, tuning deeply into their wounds, pains, joys, passions, and so on. This merging can involve temporarily becoming another through the heart where the Pisces identity merges with the identity of the other. There is always significant desire on the part of Pisces to want to heal others (including all life).

Pisces also has a natural ability, when healthy, to create a safe space for others to be vulnerable. This falls in line with possessing great interest in learning how to help and heal others through various modalities (typically related to the heart and soul). For people with Vesta in Pisces, this means holding sacred and cherishing empathy, healing, and being of service to others. This is the inner fire of one's personal temple within and can be expressed by giving as a regular theme in life, feeling into the needs of others through the heart.

VESTA IN ARIES—SACRED DEVOTION/REVERENCE FOR THE WORTHY CAUSE OR MISSION

The Aries archetype holds sacred the cause or mission worthy of full investment and attention. For people with a natal placement of Vesta in Aries, the term "all-in" becomes sacred. Aries as an archetype swirls with a restless, fiery energy always looking for something to engage in, to manifest. This archetypal energy is associated with the guardian at the gates of cosmic order (or heaven, if one prefers), or simply the warrior. But the word "warrior" has the built-in root word "war," and Aries has more concerns than just war historically.

Prior to the rise of patriarchal empires, in the first and second millennium BCE, full-time warriors or soldiers were generally a rarity. Nations, city-states, and tribes generally did not sustain year-round armies waiting to do battle. Armies were called up or raised over a finite period of time to fight in emergencies and threats to one's people or community. The Aries archetype found other important causes, such as guards (or defenders of house and family), farmers, builders, and others seeking out that which is vulnerable and in need of protecting.

After about 2000 BCE, a slow build-up of professional armies began, culminating in the Roman Empire. The Aries archetype was conscripted along with countless thousands in fighting for the nation-state regardless of one's personal beliefs. This tradition of standing armies continues into the present, with a majority of nations fielding ground, air, and sea military forces. Like many other archetypes, this use of Aries is a corruption of its original essence.

However, there are incredible examples of how Aries can show up in modern life, as in various devotions to responding to disasters and emergencies, volunteering for charitable organizations to care, heal, and defend, and simply being present for humanity in times of need. This doesn't mean Aries should not defend a nation—it's more of choice of where Aries is placing its energy. Is it worth fighting for? Is it something for which Aries can be "all-in" and feels sanguine about future results or outcomes? These questions, in relation to Vesta/Hestia, are intended to help the person see whether it is sacred to one's self or not.

Vesta in Taurus—Sacred Devotion/Reverence to the Aesthetics/Beauty/Pleasures of Earth

At least here in the Northern Hemisphere, mid-spring is the time of the great blossoming. Most life is more vibrant and colorful, generally more pleasing to all of our senses. This is the season of Taurus, representing the aesthetics, beauty, and pleasures of Earth's bounty.

One of the earliest images of Taurus is the Garden of Eden, known by many other names throughout history. The great gardens of the ancient world drew from the ancient archetypal essence of Taurus. The garden is a place where the bounty of Earth is fully realized, engaging all of our senses and tapping into the pleasure center of our being, and where sensual bliss can be experienced with Nature herself. It is the nectar of Earth come into physical form where pleasure is a goal.

Taurus has also been associated with the feminine as it was with one of the original goddesses, Inanna/Ishtar, from ancient Mesopotamia, a precursor to Venus/Aphrodite and Isis.

For people with a natal placement of Vesta in Taurus, pleasures and comforts are intended to become sacred in their life. This is about tapping into aesthetics and the five senses, engaging them in the beauty of colors, pleasant smells, and sensual touches. It is about making intimacy a sacred art and manifesting Taurus through artwork, such as foods, painting, sculpting, and gardening.

For Vesta in Taurus people, what you are experiencing is more on a physical level of pleasure, rather than mental, than the person who is connected to their own natal Taurus archetype.

VESTA IN GEMINI—SACRED DEVOTION/REVERENCE TO ETERNAL YOUTH OR FREE-ELECTRON SPIRIT[21]

The sign of Gemini is the end of spring and represents the flowering of personality in its multiple forms and overall orientation to being a free spirit. People with a natal placement of Vesta in Gemini have a sacred connection to the divine clown, exemplified by the medicine from the Lakota *heyoka* figure in the Great Plains of North America. Gemini's essence is in the *puer* or "eternal youth" archetype.

Gemini is tuned into the irreverent and the contrary to be able to experience and/or perceive from a place of freedom to do so. The purpose of the contrarian, fool, jester, or heyoka was not simply for entertainment purposes (although that was an added benefit), but to demonstrate that wisdom can come from the bizarre and a person's truth can be reflected in a Gemini figure.

For those who have Vesta in Gemini and no other personal planets or points in this sign, Gemini can show up as liberation

---

21 In *The Shamanic Astrology Handbook* (p. 28), Giamario develops the metaphor of "free electrons" from physics descriptions of electrons orbiting about the nucleus of an atom for two archetypes, Gemini and Aquarius: "Some electrons have the ability to move or jump from one atom to another and are referred to as free electrons because they can go anywhere as they are not tied to a particular atom. This imagery is opposite of a bonding electron or an electron that connects with other electrons." Thus, people with these archetypes in strategic places in the natal chart focus on being free.

beyond duality and purpose. Gemini can invite a person to experience irreverence, fun, games, and free-spirited action without attachment to an expectation or goal.

The Gemini archetype is also a shape-shifter and can be anything the imagination conceives of. Gemini can assist in shape-shifting out of intensity, tension, or perhaps an addiction to work, to (for example) sing with the birds and to simply "be" among friends *enjoying* the company but also detaching from expectations and moving beyond those moments.

Vesta in Cancer—Sacred Devotion/Reverence to Nurturing, Empathy, Compassion for the New Family, Tribe, or Community

The archetype of Cancer is the mother nurturer of the zodiac. To have Vesta in the sign of Cancer is to learn to experience what it is to have the gift of giving in a sacred manner. Inquiries into this would be "What does it mean to give?" "What does it mean to give as a higher purpose to one's self?"

These questions show up strongly when a person has nothing else in the sign of Cancer, or lacks other "giver" signs in the chart, that is, Capricorn, Virgo, and Pisces. Life's journey will provide opportunities for that person to experience Cancer in themselves as part of their overall evolution and growth as a soul in this world.

Cancer is a "middle-world" sign or archetype, meaning that it is intimately involved in the complexities of nurturing, giving, family, and desire to see that those the person cares about reach full maturation or potential. Vesta in Cancer can assist a person to obtain clues about their life purpose by giving, nurturing, and understanding what a healthy family dynamic is all about.

Vesta in Leo—Sacred Devotion/Reverence to Creative Force through Radical, Radiant Self-love

Creative force through radical, radiant self-love is what Leo is all about. Imagination and thinking big is what Leo does best. In this process, Leo tends to be a charismatic archetype that draws attention and drama to itself simply by "being." There is a part of having Vesta in Leo that involves developing a healthy ego and force of will.

When a person has Vesta in Leo, the intent is to use one's imagination, engaging in spontaneous creativity and leading with the powerful fire element of both. Radiating self-love and warmth to those around you will show the Leo coming through. If this sign (or even the element of fire) does not appear in the natal chart (or very little fire is in the chart), this placement of Vesta can make the process of shining bright a sacred process.

Vesta in Virgo—Sacred Devotion/Reverence to Co-creating and Maintaining Sacred Patterning and Rhythms of Planet/Life

Virgo is Vesta's most natural placement on the chart. Virgo as an archetype/sign represents the sacred patterns of the Earth and its relationship with us. Much of what I discussed about Vesta/Hestia pertains to Virgo. Vesta in Virgo means making the greater "pattern" itself sacred and treating one's self, body, mind, and spirit as a temple (not out of vanity, but out of reverence to creation itself).

Other notable qualities of Virgo that are intended to become sacred for a person relate to understanding the details of a pattern or rhythm and to honoring order in its balance with chaos. With Vesta in Virgo, you are also invited to treat "attention" and "focus" as something sacred in themselves. There is a certain devotion comprised of focus and attention to being of service to the cosmic order in the personal and collective lives of that which you are serving.

An example of what I am mean here comes from Jean Shinoda Bolen, MD, in *Goddesses in Everywoman*[22]: "[The virgin goddess archetype] ... focused consciousness ... [is] analogous to a sharply focused, willfully directed, intense beam of light that illuminates only what it is focused on...." Virgo can show up in life very much like this; for those who have no Virgo in their natal charts except Vesta in Virgo, it serves as a way to bring an earthy clarity into your life when necessary and honor the part of yourself that can be of service impersonally while devoting energy to the tasks at hand.

Virgo is also the most "mentally active" of the earth element signs, and this could be helpful to those who may lack the air element in the natal chart. That does not mean it is less of an earth element sign, it just means it expresses itself differently than Taurus or Capricorn, the other earth element signs.

VESTA IN LIBRA—SACRED DEVOTION/ REVERENCE TO CONSCIOUS, EQUAL RELATIONSHIPS BOTH WITHIN AND WITHOUT

Vesta's presence in Libra draws attention to the formulation of relationships going forward. What is sacred about your relationships? What about with a spouse or partner or even your own "inner other"? Are you honoring yourself in those relationships? Or are you sacrificing more than fifty percent of your being to be in that relationship? These are critical questions to those with one or more personal planets in the sign of Libra. Vesta is also a "personal planet or point" on the natal chart.

Libra as a sign/archetype is wholly concerned with relationships and knows itself through relationships of all kinds. Libra brings great attention (from a mental awareness standpoint)

---

22   Jean Shinoda Bolen, *Goddesses in Everywoman: Powerful Archetypes in Women's Lives* (New York: HarperCollins, 2014), 37.

Erik M. Roth

to building relationships, especially those that are non-hierarchical, conscious, and equal in their nature, whether romantic, intimate, friendship, work, and even family relationships. The intent of Vesta in Libra is to bring in the sacred quality to relationships in life.

In the vein of a sacred quality, it involves new training in what Libra is here to do. As Daniel Giamario writes in *The Shamanic Astrology Handbook*, "The training is about learning to give and take, being willing to be vulnerable and personal with a significant other. That is why Libra is a process-oriented path of relationship with a willingness to work on the relationship."[23]

Not only is relationship with partners quite important, but discovering who Libra is without a partner is also mandatory. The ability to connect with one's own inner beloved occurs through a process called "inner sacred marriage" by Giamario, discussed on numerous fronts in his teachings as part of the Shamanic Astrology Paradigm™.

VESTA IN SCORPIO—SACRED DEVOTION/REVERENCE TO ALIVENESS, SEXUALITY, AND PASSIONS GENERATED THROUGH WALKING ALONG THE EDGES OF CREATION

Scorpio as a sign/archetype represents the aliveness, primal energy, and vitality of the organic in ourselves and the transformation of the raw components of soil into life itself. Scorpio is about mastery of the emotional and physical domains that typically involve levels of control which at times from another's point of view can come across as detached or mysterious or even cold. But Scorpio is here is show us a path of working with chi or prana in a way that ultimately benefits us. Make no mistake, though, Scorpio is a sign that operates through self-interest or self-exploration. As a water element sign, it is certainly capable of *feeling* compassion and empathy, but it works with it

---

23   Giamario, *The Shamanic Astrology Handbook*, 63.

very differently than the other water signs Cancer and Pisces. Scorpio's role is to turn itself on through the juiciness of life.

There is much to the sign of Scorpio that remained hidden for centuries following the rise of combined monotheistic and patriarchal cultures because Scorpio was deeply connected to the feminine mysteries. Part of what Vesta in Scorpio can represent is a reframing and return to the feminine mysteries without the fear and judgment of patriarchal culture.

Having Vesta in Scorpio makes sacred that which is important to Scorpio, namely, opening to the universal chi or prana and feeling the aliveness for its own sake. Honoring self in feeling one's own vitality and aliveness is critical to knowing Scorpio. Scorpio is also the "edgewalker," and it is drawn toward taking things to the edge of life and death and beyond in order to know what the edge is and where it is located.

What is the nature of personal power? Vesta in Scorpio is here to inquire about that very question. This is not exploration of the illusion of power over others (which can be a shadow for Scorpio), but power within self in the process of mastery (not to become someone's "master"). Perhaps it is a mastery of an art that involves chi such as a martial art form or a form of yoga. Perhaps it is mastery through athletics or being in a position of power in the corporate, political, or social world. Perhaps it is mastery of willpower in self in all aspects of life or all of the above.

VESTA IN SAGITTARIUS—SACRED DEVOTION/ REVERENCE TO MEANING AND TRUTH THROUGH EXPLORING NEW FRONTIERS

The Sagittarius sign/archetype's role is exploration of meaning and truth as its primary motivation. Sagittarius is a highly active and fiery force or restless energy that desires to be on the go, to see what is new and blaze new trails in life. Sagittarius thrives when it is on the move or on the search for something beyond itself. In ancient times, this sign related to the trail scout of the tribe or perhaps the trader along the Silk Road. In more recent times, the Sagittarius spirit has been an explorer of continents across the oceans and rocketing to space and the Moon.

The Sagittarius archetype is not concerned with the complexities of family or routine except as a waystation to new frontiers. As one of the four signs/archetypes "in service to spirit," it accomplishes this through explorations of meaning and truth as the highest calling. Sagittarius is called not just to the ends of the Earth, but to those of the mind and spirit as well.

Having Vesta in this sign will have you treating the search for meaning as a sacred gift to yourself and serving spirit while doing so. It can mean that the seeker part of you goes to the highest and most distant tangible and intangible places in order to see or envision the widest possible horizons.

Vesta and the Twelve Astrological Houses

I n addition to the sign where Vesta resides, it is important to include its house position in the natal chart. In brief, the houses represent the personal environment that a particular planet inhabits (or that of the Moon, Sun, Angle, other points). This astrological environment helps express the qualities of the sign and planet, primarily on a more *progressive* or forward-moving level. This means the astrological house is part of the leading-edge expression of the sign and planet (or Moon, Sun, Angle). The astrological house adds a deeper element to the chart and its interpretation. In this section, I provide a summary for each of the twelve houses through the lens of shamanic astrology.

Each of the twelve houses has a deep resonance with an astrological sign or archetype, which gives the planet and sign in a particular house greater complexity and potential qualities that may not have been evident when focusing on planetary signs alone. The first and eighth through the twelfth astrological houses are always above the horizon regardless of where a person is born on the planet. Houses two through seven are below the horizon, again, no matter the location of one's birth. However, the first and seventh, which determine the Ascendant and Descendant, could be interpreted as "in between" the visible and invisible in that they are on the eastern and western horizons, respectively. Astrological software calculates the houses according to a particular house system. The Shamanic Astrology Paradigm™ utilizes the whole-sign house system. Table 3 summarizes the characteristics and resonant archetype/sign for each house.

Table 3: Meanings of the Astrological Houses

House	Characteristics, keywords	Archetype/sign resonance with
First	Self-identity, early life, body, being all-in vis-à-vis chosen, passionately held commitment	Aries
Second	Receiving, pleasure, sensuality, livelihood, material circumstances	Taurus
Third	Communication, perception, youth/play, siblings, mind/mental activity	Gemini
Fourth	Home, family, roots, parents, nurturing, how one feels at home	Cancer
Fifth	Creativity, children, romance, radical and radiant self-love	Leo
Sixth	Sacredness and sacred space, grand design patterning, health, service	Virgo
Seventh	Conscious and equal partnership or simply relationship; on the "relationship axis" or polarity with first house of identity	Libra
Eighth	Death and rebirth, transformation, empowerment	Scorpio
Ninth	Vision quest and exploration of truth and meaning, loosely related to travel	Sagittarius
Tenth	Constructed reality and expression in the world; career, social position	Capricorn
Eleventh	Consciousness and cosmic or higher awareness beyond linear 3D reality, friendships, associations, aspirations	Aquarius
Twelfth	Subconscious, dreams, underworld, and cosmic heart or oneness of all	Pisces

Vesta in First House

Having Vesta in the first house sets the intent of the Vesta archetype to be completely aligned with one's emerging identity. Since the Ascendant is always in the first house, this can lead to less ambiguity between one's sacred inner hearth and personal identity project. Vesta will take on a greater supporting role, emphasizing the Ascendant in helping to maximize life rewards via ever greater experiences surrounding the archetype of one's natal Ascendant.

Vesta in Second House

Vesta in the second house creates a personal application to more of the pleasure center as the expression of the natal Vesta archetype. The second house's essence, similar to Taurus, is about the "savoring the pleasures of life" and "slowing down to appreciate those pleasures." In the material world, this can lead to creating more security to protect those pleasures.

Vesta in Third House

For a person born with Vesta in the third house, and like the sign of Gemini, there is an emphasis on communication, imagination, fun, socialization, and mental processes. The natal Vesta archetype will be directed toward those qualities with an intent to experience extroversion and dialogue with others. This house helps open up the personality more freely.

Vesta in Fourth House

This house is about home and family and the responsibilities to maintain and nurture the home and family. Home and family is broadly defined here and does not directly refer to traditional households. Having Vesta in the fourth house is an underlying environment toward experiencing the Vesta archetype around the household and family/friends. This house has many qualities that are similar to the sign of Cancer.

VESTA IN FIFTH HOUSE

Vesta in the fifth house conveys a youthful, creative spirit to the natal Vesta archetype. The fifth house is a dynamic, fiery-spirited and intuitive environment and can draw drama to the person with personal planets located there. This house is Leo-like in its expression and can help motivate a person to be a leader, to share their big dreams and visions and shine the light of radical, radiant self-love upon the dark.

VESTA IN SIXTH HOUSE

The sixth house is similar in its expression to the sign of Virgo and helps a person explore the sacred within. For people with Vesta in the sixth house, this helps bring in an amplified (due to Vesta itself symbolizing that already and being Virgo-like) sacredness and detail orientation to their natal Vesta archetype.

VESTA IN SEVENTH HOUSE

Having Vesta in the seventh house sets an intent for the person to integrate the Vesta archetype into relationships. In the natal chart, the Descendant is always located in this house and so will be influenced by Vesta and vice versa (Descendant will also influence Vesta). The Descendant represents "relationship intent" and, like Vesta, it depends on the archetype present in the seventh house. Vesta in the seventh house will assist a person in learning the most from relationships, particularly intimate ones.

VESTA IN EIGHTH HOUSE

This is the house of death and rebirth and hence soulful transformation. Vesta in the eighth house assists a person in experiencing the archetype here in a deeper, more transformative way than other houses. The placement of Vesta here can be initially challenging and potentially fearful in getting to know this archetype consciously, but with maturity the Vesta archetype can help connect one to glimpses of buried treasures within the soul.

Vesta in Ninth House

This is the house of adventures and explorations of meaning and truth. The ninth house is similar to the sign of Sagittarius, and those born with Vesta in this house experience a more expansive perception of the life journey. The natal Vesta archetype in this house assists in expanding beyond its regular expression by adding a touch of Sagittarius to the archetype.

Vesta in Tenth House

For a person with Vesta in the tenth house, a constructive, practical approach is created to experience the natal Vesta archetype. The tenth house is about one's calling or vocation in the 3D world and has a great deal of resonance with the sign of Capricorn. The environment of the tenth house can assist a person with Vesta located here to experience Vesta as something useful in life that can help grow and utilize resources (monetary or otherwise), which will involve one's work or life calling or both.

Vesta in Eleventh House

The eleventh house of the astrology chart, like Aquarius, represents the expansion of consciousness, idealism, innovation, eccentricity, and the global community. For a person with Vesta here, there is an intent to apply the archetype to a broader scale with a more celestial approach in being able to see the human collective as a whole. This house will also innovate the natal Vesta archetype toward a more radical version of itself.

Vesta in Twelfth House

Similar to Pisces, the twelfth house opens the heart and spirit somewhat hidden from the mundane world. The twelfth is also the house of the subconscious and dream world. For a person with Vesta in this house, it can take more years to experience the archetype's fullness than in any other house. But this house also shares what the Vesta archetype present here will have added to it—empathy, compassion, and spiritual openness.

How the Planets, Sun, Moon, and Nodes Interact with Vesta

The Sun, Moon, and other planets in the solar system can play major roles in how the natal Vesta position expresses itself in a person's life. Discussion in this section is more advanced, especially in relation to the astrological aspects. The interactions between planets or the Sun, Moon, and so on, are highly complex, but a general essence or concept can be seen in how each of them interacts with Vesta, the large asteroid (nearly as massive as a dwarf planet).

The strongest relationship I have discovered is between Saturn and Vesta, as described in the section titled "Vesta's Relationship with Saturn." Note that both celestial bodies were named for deities that represented form and order. At their core, the two can assist each other in creating a healthy balance in many areas of life, spiritual expression in the 3D world, and promoting humanity's understanding of the flow of greater patterns in time, such as in the life span, middle world, right use of resources, economics, politics, relationships, daily life routines, and astronomy.

In the following, I begin with the other outer planets and work toward the inner solar system, including the dwarf planet Ceres. It's also worth keeping in mind that planetary aspects to Vesta are not as significant as aspects to "personal" bodies in the solar system—Moon, Sun, Mercury, Venus, or Mars.

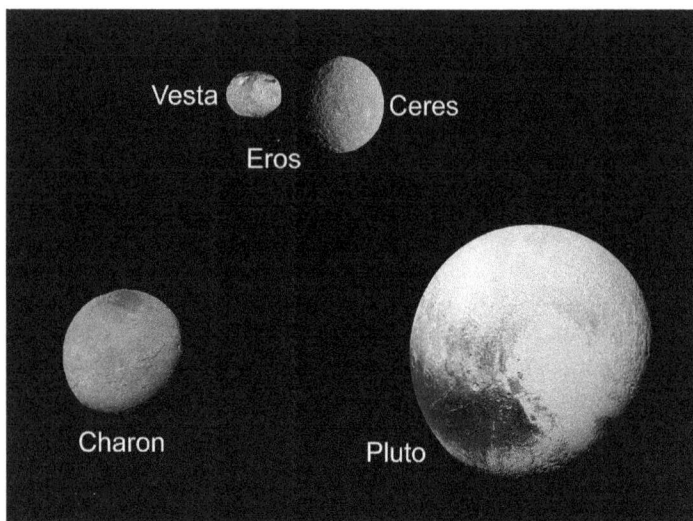

The asteroids Ceres, Vesta, and Eros compared to the sizes of Pluto and its moon Charon. Ceres is by far the largest object found within the asteroid belt, and the only object within the region known to be in hydrostatic equilibrium. It is smaller and less massive than Charon. If all of the mass found within the asteroid belt were to be clumped together, it would be roughly twice as massive as Charon.

Image credit: Ceres image: Justin CowartEros image: NASA/JPLVesta image: NASA/JPL-Caltech/UCAL/MPS/ DLR/IDAPluto and Charon images: NASA/Johns Hopkins University Applied Physics Laboratory/Southwest Research Institute/Alex Parker / Public domain

PLUTO AND VESTA

When Pluto is in a dynamic aspect ("hard" aspect in Western astrology) with Vesta in the natal chart, it adds an element of the underworld to the chart (i.e., the person's life). The underworld is not a bad or evil place as certain religions suggest. In this "place," human beings experience the raw, primal energy of creation and chaos, which has no connection to the rational mind or intellect. Here we surrender to our higher selves and the driving forces of creation itself. The underworld is not a puzzle we can solve. The only truly healthy decision we can make is to participate in the process so as to understand our feelings, fears, and pains.

This combination of Pluto and Vesta (depending on the sign and house position Vesta is located in) is akin to a Scorpio overlay in the chart. (Pluto creates an infusion of Scorpio into personal planets, including Vesta, and this can lead to a Scorpio overlay of a person's natal Vesta sign.) For persons with this dynamic aspect (as well as no personal planets in Scorpio), Pluto and Vesta instill qualities of the Scorpio archetype. The intent or meaning of this combination is to make the underworld a sacred ally or area in one's life.

The Pluto–Vesta pattern is not as regular as Saturn–Vesta. The most notable periods of Vesta's orbital relationship with Pluto are when Vesta spends several months in the same sign in and around its retrograde period. During this time, Vesta can have a series of three conjunctions with Pluto over 6 to 8 months. Regardless of whether each is a square, opposition, or a conjunction, it means Pluto plays a more significant role in a person's life with the archetype intended to become sacred (natal Vesta sign).

When I describe Pluto to people, I say that this dwarf planet is akin to the deep, dark, and rich soil of the Earth where the decay of matter has taken place and composted into its base minerals and nutrients. The death and thus composting of assorted plants and animals becomes what is needed for birthing new life.

Following is a list from 1819 to 2085 of 6- to 8-month periods of three Vesta–Pluto conjunctions. *Vesta and Pluto pass through long periods with several triple conjunctions, and then much longer periods without any triple conjunctions.*

1819–1972: No triple conjunctions.

1973–1974: Two triple conjunctions in Libra, one in December 1973 and the other in April–May 1974.

1985: Three triple conjunctions in Scorpio, one each in February, March, and July.

1986–2083: No triple conjunctions.

2084–2085: Two triple conjunctions in Aries, one in August–September 2084 and the other in January 2085.

NEPTUNE AND VESTA

One of the two celestial-world planets, Neptune is the outermost planet in the solar system (according to the International Astronomical Union, which relegated Pluto to dwarf planet status in 2006). In shamanic astrology, Neptune has qualities that represent nonlinear time: the vast celestial sea, dreams, the unconscious, and our heart-centered and mystical connection to all in our environment. Neptune in one's life creates a theme of the dream-walk into the mystical part of our nature, the intangible and non-physical in life. It is the mirage, illusion, and the sense of being lost and confused. Neptune's intent or action helps dissolve what no longer serves in our lives; becoming confused helps our opening up to the next stage in our soul journey.

Having Vesta with Neptune in a natal square, conjunction, or opposition adds the qualities above in an alchemical joining with the Vesta sign/archetype. If we find ourselves increasingly conditioned in a consumption-driven world in Western culture, having a strong Neptune influence in our chart or even in an aspect with Vesta can challenge us to participate fully in the world while simultaneously motivating us to dream into other realms. Like Pluto and Uranus, Neptune plays an enormous role in human beings' connection with the vastness of life and the depth of the soul.

A Neptune–Vesta dynamic aspect can create detachment from the natal Vesta sign that is intended to become sacred. A person can feel as if Vesta's qualities are just out of reach when seeing glimpses of the same and briefly experiencing it. Neptune's intent here is to allow a broader, heart-centered, and dream-like approach to experiencing the natal Vesta sign.

An example is a person born with Neptune in conjunction with natal Vesta in Aries. Because the essence of Aries has a tendency toward straightforward, black-and-white perception, Neptune can present a "washout" of those qualities. In other words, the Aries connection to mission-oriented, decisive, and actional qualities manifesting the sacred in life becomes difficult with Neptune in conjunction. A different kind of Aries would evolve from a Neptune–Vesta conjunction (or opposition, square) than the average Aries (i.e., Aries without any outer planet aspects).

Neptune fully completes its transit around the Sun in 165 years. Vesta moves into a conjunction (or square, opposition) every 3.1 years, and a dynamic aspect with Neptune occurs about every 9 months. During two complete trips around the Sun for Neptune, Vesta averages 106 conjunctions. But there are short periods of time during which Neptune and Vesta have a series of three conjunctions; these periods are quite rare as both objects have to be retrograde at the same time during part of the transit. Following are the years when the three-conjunction series occurs:

1740–1741: September and December 1740, April 1741 in Cancer

1789: January, April, and June in Libra

1800: February, April, and August in Scorpio

1870: June, November, and December in Aries

1907–1908: October 1907, January and April 1908 in Cancer

1967: February, May, and July in Scorpio

1978: March, May, and September in Sagittarius

2037: July, November, and December in Aries

2048–2049: September and October 2048, and March 2049 in Taurus

URANUS AND VESTA

With a combination of archetypal forces in Prometheus and the Sky God, Uranus is seen as a great wildcard among the planets. Having Uranus and Vesta in conjunction, square, or opposition to each other in the natal chart creates an intention for Vesta archetypal and house qualities to be expressed in a revolutionary and unorthodox way. Uranus paves the way for a sudden (sometimes, dramatic), unexpected, and novel theme in a person's life. This aspect comprises an injection of Aquarian qualities into Vesta, giving one's natal Vesta motivation for expanding consciousness and gaining a bigger-picture perspective.

Uranus is part of the celestial (aka upper) world. Giamario[24] provides a description of this planetary vibration as a blowtorch going up and out into the heavens (compared to Pluto's moving down and into the core). Having Uranus in a dynamic aspect to one's natal Vesta provides for a more radical version of that archetype (and house) to be expressed as sacred.

An example is a person whose natal Vesta is in the sign of Leo and in conjunction with Uranus. This combination creates a spark-filled, self-loving, dramatic, and consciousness-expanding creative vibration that is intended to be held sacred within. In addition, this person would experience unexpected

---

24 Giamario, *The Shamanic Astrology Handbook*.

shifts in life to expand their consciousness and allow greater exploration of radical, radiant self-love for its own sake. Adding an astrological house with a different wavelength would of course change this a bit. An example would be a person born with Vesta in the sign of Leo and the fourth house in the natal chart. This would involve adding a layer to Vesta's expression that is about family activities, nurture, and compassion. Then we add Uranus as a sudden and unexpected shock or lightning bolt to Vesta's expression, creating a highly unique sacredness of Leo and family dynamics—it would be unconventional and prone to sharp and dramatic changes.

Uranus takes 84 years to return to its starting place in a given natal chart, which is why a Uranus return occurs at age 83–84. Vesta will be in one of four dynamic aspects to Uranus an average of 26 to 27 times over one complete orbital passage of Uranus or 53 times over two complete orbital passages of Uranus.

Compared to Vesta's triple-conjunction series with Pluto and Neptune, these interactions with Uranus are even more rare. In the past 120 years, only two triple conjunctions of Vesta and Uranus took place; another will occur 46 years after the last one in 1989.

1943–1944: August 1943 and January and February 1944 in Gemini

1989: April, July, and September in Capricorn

2034–2035: September 2034, and January and March 2035 in Cancer

Chiron and Vesta

In 1977, a new type of cosmological body identified by astronomers became known as centaurs. Hence, the first centaur-type body was named Chiron. Centaur mythology is thousands of years old, with Chiron as a rare figure in that he was a healer, astronomer, astrologer, and teacher. In shamanic astrology, Chiron represents human beings' fracture points and wounds. Interpretation is primarily dependent on Chiron's resident astrological house and the personal planets and points that it aspects at birth. If Chiron is in dynamic (hard) aspect to Vesta at the time of birth, it gives that person significant clues about the nature of their wounds.

The most common fractures for humans involve betrayal, perfectionism, guilt and shame, abandonment, and victimization (as outlined by Giamario in the *Shamanic Astrology Handbook*). For Chiron in dynamic aspect to Vesta, the fracture can be something that a person is intended to hold as sacred in their life. It has a specific archetypal quality that becomes an area of vulnerability.

For example, a client I will call Steven was born with Vesta in Cancer and Chiron in the third house in a natal square with Vesta (Chiron is also in conjunction with his natal South Node). This presents a deeply specific intention for him to experience the power of the fracture around nurturing, providing safe space and responsible parenting grounded in compassion, love, and empathy. Steven experienced very little love from others growing up, but more importantly, from himself, and had difficulty communicating this. Later, he was able to turn this fracture/wound into something sacred in his new family while learning empathy, compassion, and self-love. While this example does not encompass other factors in Steven's astrology chart, it provides an opportunity to view a major clue regarding the fractures and wounds he chose to work with.

Chiron has a more elliptical orbit than does Uranus and Neptune, and returns to its starting place on average every 50 years (every 48-½ to 51 years). During four complete orbits of Chiron around the Sun (200 years) and back to the same place in Earth's sky, Vesta and Chiron experience 59 conjunctions, which equates to once every 3.4 years. This creates an average dynamic-aspect pattern of a conjunction, square, opposition, and second square occurring nearly once per calendar year.

Appearing next is a short list of years and months for Chiron–Vesta triple conjunctions between 1860 and 2060. Both objects must be retrograde together during a period when three conjunctions take place during a 6-month timeframe.

1860–1884: No triple conjunctions

1885–1886: August 1885, and January and February 1886 in Gemini

1893–1894: December 1893, and February and June 1894 in Virgo

1895–1931: No triple conjunctions

1932–1933: August and December 1932, and January 1933 in Taurus

1933–1978: No triple conjunctions

1979–1980: August and October 1979 and February 1980 in Taurus

1981–2123: No triple conjunctions

Prior to the above dates, in the 1660–1860 period the triple conjunctions took place seven times. As seen here, Chiron's elliptical orbit contributes to the irregularity of this pattern.

Saturn and Vesta

Saturn's contributions to a person's Vesta placement are extensive, especially when the natal Saturn is in a dynamic relationship (conjunction, opposition, or square) with Vesta. When Saturn is involved with Vesta via square, conjunction, or opposition, a person's natal archetype for Vesta will be about growth through overcoming limits and boundaries. Next, Saturn will inject more of the earth elemental qualities into that archetype, making it constructive and practical in its expression. Saturn can bring in more of a sense of right and wrong with the laws and rules of humanity, and combined with Vesta, makes that approach/expression sacred.

Because Saturn has a 29-½–year orbit and eight orbits of Vesta are equal to almost precisely 29 years, they are more intimately connected with each other than other Vesta–planet combinations. This relationship is compounded when Vesta and Saturn have three successive conjunctions in a period of less than 6 months, which provides for a more substantial inquiry into what Saturn brings to a person's life if she happens to be born during one of those time periods.

Three successive conjunctions took place relatively frequently in the 1600s (five times), 1700s (seven times), and 1800s (six times). In the 20th century, a triple conjunction happened only three times; the same number of triples will take place in the 21st century. In the last 80 years, Saturn and Vesta experienced a triple conjunction once (in 1939, in Taurus and Aries) and will not recur until 2030–2031. In the 2200s, a triple will happen only once.

Jupiter and Vesta

A person born with Jupiter and Vesta in a dynamic aspect can expect an expansion of Vesta's archetype in the natal chart. Jupiter acts as an agent of expansion to whatever it touches on the chart. If Jupiter and Vesta share the same sign/archetype in the natal chart, then Vesta becomes a major key for the individual's vision quest or path of spirituality.

If the chart is perceived as a vehicle/vessel, then Jupiter is the road or seaway that the vehicle travels. Jupiter plays a critical role in a person's chart for understanding life direction, and can serve as a compass for where life rewards manifest. It represents the *how* in getting to know the Ascendant (Rising Sign). That is because the Ascendant symbolizes not only a person's beginner status (archetypally speaking) in a given lifetime, but also what the new story is built on (the old story comes from the lineage symbolized by the Moon sign).

A Vesta–Jupiter conjunction in the same sign is a highly significant alignment in the chart for determining life purpose. Squares and oppositions between Vesta and Jupiter also create valuable insights in how Vesta contributes to life purpose, as seen below in Whitney Houston's chart (Fig. 2) and the explanation of the alignment.

Jupiter takes about 12 months to pass through a single sign and thus about 12 years to pass through all the signs. Conjunctions, oppositions, and squares typically happen less often between Vesta and Jupiter in a natal chart. In the 50-year period between 1980 and 2030, there are 10 conjunctions between Jupiter and Vesta (about once every 5 years). In that same period, there are 34 squares (17 squares between each conjunction and opposition of Jupiter and Vesta) and 17 oppositions.

From 1950 to 2050, there are 21 conjunctions, and at one point a series of three conjunctions between December 2038 and May 2039 in the signs of Virgo and Leo. The last time that happened was in 1766–1767 when a series of three conjunctions took place in the sign of Virgo. In the 1700–2050 period, a series of three conjunctions between Jupiter and Vesta takes place only three times. When a Vesta–Jupiter conjunction (within 10 degrees) occurs in the natal chart, it signifies that Vesta plays a critical role in understanding life purpose. Note that Vesta in conjunction with the North Node, Ascendant, or Midheaven (Mc) is similarly critical in determining a person's life purpose.

Jupiter–Vesta oppositions and squares are also important in interpreting life direction, but with a bit more complexity than a same-sign conjunction. An example of this is the American singer and actress Whitney Houston (1963–2012), born with Vesta in Libra (in the eighth house) and Jupiter in Aries in opposition (see Fig. 2). The most significant quality of this particular opposition was played out in the rocky relationship with her husband Bobby Brown.

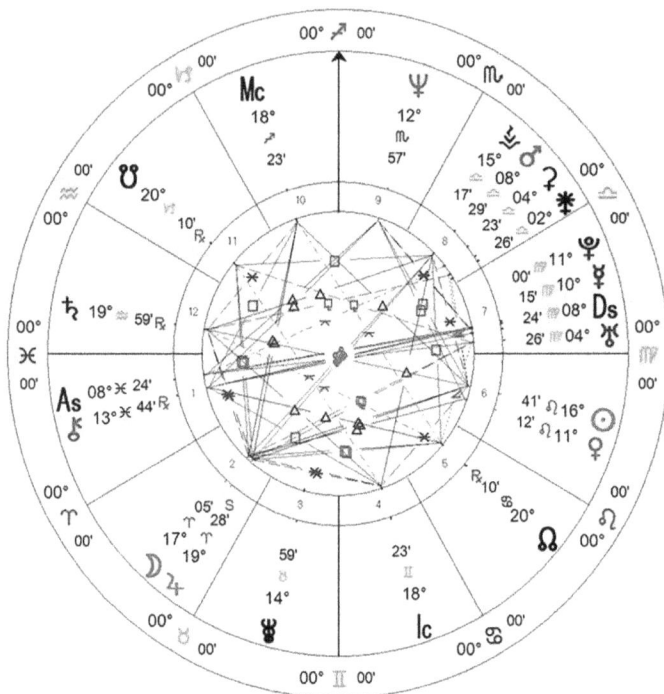

Whitney Houston
Natal Chart
Aug 9 1963, Fri
8:55 pm +4:00
Newark, New Jersey
40°N44'08" 074°W10'22"
Geocentric
Tropical
Whole Signs
True Node
Rating: AA

Fig. 2. Natal chart for Whitney Houston.

In addition to Vesta in Libra, she also had Mars, Juno, and Ceres in the same sign. I believe the most important contribution from Jupiter here is its expansion of her relationship to the masculine, how she defined relationship, and how important and sacred it was to her. These qualities strongly showed up in her music as she truly longed for an ideal relationship with the masculine. This was compounded by the fact that when she was born, Pluto was conjunct Mercury and her Descendant in the seventh house (representing relationship intent). The intent of all of this is to explore the great depths and transformation of relationship at its deepest level.

What Vesta brought to the picture was a great appreciation of the sovereignty of relationship, but also of challenges involved in letting go of a toxic partnership. This was evidenced in Diane Sawyer's 2002 interview of Houston as she discussed her trials with Bobby Brown and drug use for many years.

VESTA AND CERES

During a presentation at a Shamanic Astrology Mystery School event in February 2019, Gael Chilson, a healer and astrologer from Arizona, demonstrated the importance of this dwarf planet in our lives. Ceres is slowly becoming a part of the Shamanic Astrology Paradigm™, and in my view, like Vesta, Ceres is already part of it.

Ceres represents the Great Mother and is connected to our relationship with our human mother as well. There is a little overlap with Venus in this regard, but Ceres adds an element dealing with myth/story of Ceres and Persephone and the takeover by the patriarchy of the old order from the matriarchy and matrilineal cultures in combination with rigid monotheistic religions/cults. Ceres is connected to

Ceres; A model for a marble statuette, formerly owned by the duc de Choiseul, now in the Louvre, Paris.
Photo by Augustin Pajou / CC0

Gaia or Mother Earth (which is what I generally mean by the term "Great Mother").

Ceres is not considered to be an "outer" planet like Saturn, Uranus, Neptune, or Pluto. It is rather an "inner" planet, in that this terrestrial/rocky type of planet is inside Jupiter's orbit, and thus becomes more of a "personal" planet (Venus, Mercury, and Mars are personal planets; the Sun and Moon, although not planets, are personal points in an astrology chart).

If a person has Vesta and Ceres in conjunction, there is a magical transmission that combines the sacredness of that specific archetype (in the same sign) with the Great Mother and Persephone myth. The meaning of such conjunction is highly dependent on the archetype they carry in the chart, as well as the house. The importance of the conjunction increases when another planet or the Sun or Moon are conjunct with the Vesta–Ceres pair.

As seen in the following listing, the two "asteroids" coming together in conjunction is much more infrequent than any other Vesta combination with an outer planet. Ceres takes 4.6 years to complete an orbit and spends about 3 months in the same sign. Vesta completes an orbit in 3.6 years and spends 2-½ to 3 months in a given sign. In the 500-year span of 1700–2200 CE, the two asteroids conjunct with each other 29 times. In even more rare situations, as summarized below, due to respective orbits, a series of three conjunctions occurs (all time periods are common era).

92–93: 1 conjunction each in Aries, Taurus, and Cancer

589–590: 2 conjunctions in Aries and 1 in Cancer

915: 3 conjunctions in Aquarius

1087–1088: 1 conjunction each in Taurus, Cancer, and Leo

1584–1585: 1 conjunction in Taurus and 2 conjunctions in Cancer

2578–2579: 3 conjunctions in Gemini

2887–2888: 1 conjunction each in Cancer, Leo, and Libra

Celebrities born during a Vesta–Ceres conjunction include Jodie Foster, Bette Midler, Jim Carrey, Steve Martin, Wayne Gretzky, Katie Holmes, Barrack Obama, Diana (Princess of Wales), and Goldie Hawn.

However, there are even more rare events when a conjunction, square, or opposition is equivalent to a longer period of more than three in the series. This happens more frequently (than the Vesta–Ceres conjunctions) when Ceres and Vesta are in polarity (opposition) to one another. A series of nine exact oppositions occurred between July 1968 and April 1973 in multiple signs. In the near future, a series of seven oppositions between October 2020 and May 2024 will occur. So, what do these more frequent oppositions mean?

For people born in one of those longer periods where Vesta and Ceres are in opposition with each other, it means the two celestial bodies highlight each other, bringing illumination to their respective archetypes. The gifts of those archetypes tend to show up as reflective of that polarity.

As mentioned earlier for Vesta alone, the two asteroids in relationship are not as prominent in a person's life as Venus, the Moon, Sun, Mars, Mercury, or Jupiter. But they can augment a person's spiritual depth. Celebrities who were born with Ceres and Vesta in opposition include Kevin Costner, Cary Grant, Dustin Hoffman, Mary Tyler Moore, Annie Lennox, and Denzel Washington.

MARS AND VESTA

Mars represents the emergent masculine principle in shamanic astrology, which is somewhat different from what other schools of astrology teach about the red planet. In my experience, the evidence about Mars and its relationship with the masculine is fairly clear. The masculine shows up very strongly, of course, in men, but we see the masculine in women as well and other genders. Mars does not make a person male; rather, it shows how masculinity is expressed and tends to be more strongly personal in men than other genders.

Mars also has a physical component in men that I've noticed over years of performing astrology readings. Its archetypal vulnerabilities can show up in conditions and physical activities, especially during planetary transits (cycles).

For women, in general, Mars represents the archetype they are longing for in life, and while it is usually in the form a romantic/intimate partner, it can be anything that archetype symbolizes. In transgender people, it varies on a case-by-case basis.

When a person has Mars and Vesta together in a dynamic aspect in the natal chart, it means that Vesta provides a significant influence in how Mars is expressed. An example is the chart of Jim Morrison, the musician, singer, and poet of the rock band, The Doors. Jim was born on December 8, 1943, during a close conjunction of Vesta and Mars in the sign of Gemini in the fifth house. In addition, the birth occurred during a very rare setup with Uranus, Vesta, and Mars all conjunct and retrograde, and just after the time when the Sun was in opposition to each of those three planetary bodies in Gemini. This means they were all rising around the same time as the Sun (in Sagittarius) was setting.

For Jim, the Mars–Vesta (and Uranus) conjunction in Gemini made for incredible expression of his sacred rhythm and tuning in on a personal level through his music and other creative work. He enjoyed breaking all the rules in music and stagecraft, using his physical presence to embody the trickster in unexpected ways—and all the while not caring what people thought of him. He was a shapeshifter playing many roles within the guise of a musician. Creativity oozed from him in unpredictable ways while staying in the body of his Taurus Moon (i.e., he enjoyed the pleasures of his physical form and was able to experience it on a new level with the Mars–Vesta conjunction).

Gemini became a sacred expression as it related to the masculine. The conventional and stereotypical masculine was turned on its head in Morrison who was never afraid to display himself unclothed on stage when public nudity was against the law; he knew he would be led off-stage by security or police, and laughed in delight at the attention, the sheer glory of acting out. He rarely had trouble being himself, but was challenged by 3D reality, which led to his early death at age 27.

Another example is Valerie, a client I worked with over a two-year period. She was born with Vesta in the sign of Libra, and Mars in the sign of Scorpio, with the Sun between the two celestial bodies. Added to this was a complex factor of the planet Neptune also in conjunction with her natal Mars. Scorpio initially becomes or represents the partner she wants. Later in life, especially during the mid-life passage, the tendency became more about taking ownership of the Scorpio projections and developing her inner Scorpio beloved/lover.

But with Vesta in the sign of Libra, a part of her is looking to have conscious, equal partnership as something sacred, a blessing. The signs Libra and Scorpio have little in common. Scorpio is the edge-walker, intense, and willful, the one who directs the chi and tends to be more "alpha-like" in relationships. Valerie may feel attracted to partners who lack conscious, equal partnership as a priority in their lives.

With Neptune also conjunct with Valerie's Mars, she can be led down a road of romantic idealization of the relationship she desires as sacred but which becomes an illusion. The solution is to develop a relationship with her inner masculine, a process called the "inner sacred marriage process" in the Shamanic Astrology Paradigm™. This is a process of creation and dialogue with the inner masculine, which is a key component toward the path of wholeness. As suggested here, Vesta contributes much to a person's life by adding a layer of sacred to that which each unique being is working on in life.

Since Mars orbits closer to Vesta than any other planet, save for the dwarf planet Ceres, these two celestial planets have a more unique dance with each other than the outer planets. On average, there is an exact conjunction between Mars and Vesta nearly every 47 months. Mars and Vesta had a triple conjunction only five times in a 1,900-year period. The last time was in 1943–1944 in Gemini (*when Jim Morrison was born*). The next time will occur in 2787, also in Gemini.

In contrast to triple conjunctions, there are numerous series of three oppositions and squares between Mars and Vesta. The last series of three squares took place in 1999–2000 and the next time this occurs is 2020–2021. Between 1900 and 2200 there are 26 occurrences of a triple-square series and 29 oppositions.

VENUS AND VESTA

Representing the emergent feminine principle, the second planet from the Sun named for the Roman goddess of love, Venus carries an ancient lineage that has helped human beings understand themselves in relation to the cosmos. Like the masculine principle, feminine expression has 12 archetypal expressions. The feminine shows up more strongly, of course, in women but is within all other genders as well. Venus also has a physical component in women that I have noticed through years of giving astrology readings in that its archetypal vulnerabilities can show up in physical conditions and activities, especially during planetary transits (cycles).

For men, Venus generally represents the archetype they are longing for in life, and while it is usually in the form a romantic/intimate partner, it can be anything that the archetype symbolizes. In transgender people, it will vary on a case-by-case basis.

When a person has Venus and Vesta together in a dynamic aspect, it means that Vesta provides a significant influence on how Venus is expressed in the chart. An example is Samantha, a client who was born with Vesta and Venus in conjunction in Virgo. Her expression of the feminine in the current lifetime is intended to be in honor of the sacred and being of service to

Marble head from a portrait statue of a veiled priestess of the goddess Vesta, Roman Empire, British Museum.

Photo by Carole Raddato from FRANKFURT, Germany / CC BY-SA

the cosmic order. In more specific language, she is drawn to treating herself as a complex sacred being and to creating sacred space in her home and more broadly in her personal life, including intimate relationships.

Vesta in conjunction with Venus enforces the need for Samantha to honor the emergent Virgo nature in her life. It is important for her to deeply understand the greater life pattern (primarily her own), work with the nuances and details of her life pattern, and to be of service to a greater order in life. This Vesta–Venus conjunction in Virgo indicates that Samantha is evolving into a more complex person as her own pattern emerges into the archetype of the priestess (Virgo). An alignment like this can create a personal need to serve with sacred work, that is, dedication to and giving to something important in life. Virgo is the archetype of the priestess and having a role where that personal archetype can express itself is vital to Samantha's personal growth in both the feminine and the sacred hearth within.

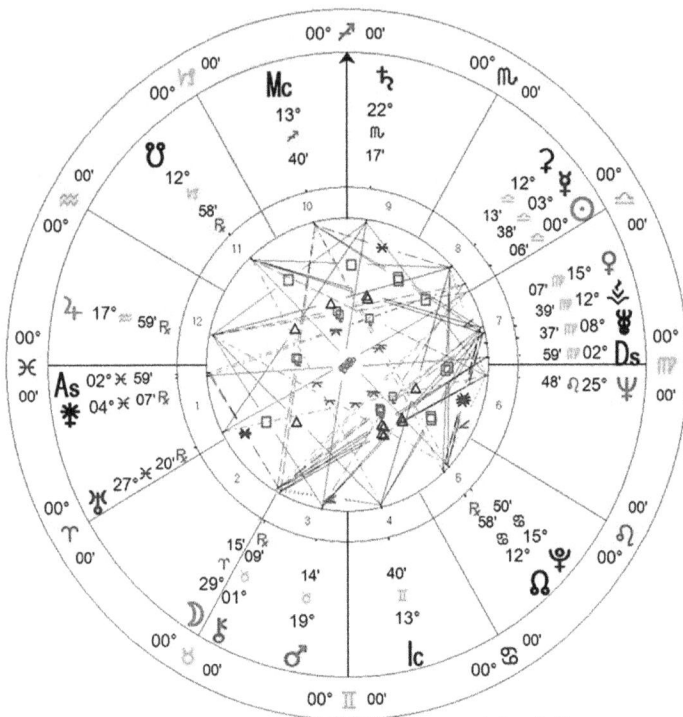

Fig. 3. Natal chart for John Coltrane

John Coltrane
Male Chart
Sep 23 1926, Thu
5:00 pm EST +5:00
Hamlet, NC
34°N53'05" 079°W41'40"
Geocentric
Tropical
Whole Signs
True Node
Rating: AA

Another example here is John Coltrane, born September 23, 1926, with a Venus–Vesta conjunction in Virgo in the seventh house (see Fig. 3). He made a powerful imprint in American jazz in the 1950s and 1960s. Coltrane's music was his love, his priestess. The complex patterns of the music, that is, its sacredness, and his relationship with jazz were a powerful way for his inner feminine to express itself.

Virgo as an archetype can turn a person's dedication into something spiritual and Coltrane released many songs later in life (before dying in 1967 at age 40) that contained a sense of the spiritual. He was born with a Pisces Ascendant, which really began to show itself in his thirties, and was certainly showing up in his musical creations and spiritual pursuits.

Other well-known celebrities with Vesta–Venus conjunctions include George Harrison, Ringo Starr, Charlie Chaplin, Melissa Ethridge, Tracey Ullman, and Abraham Lincoln.

Vesta and Venus have conjunctions, oppositions, and squares nearly every year with one another and in certain years have a series of three conjunctions. Vesta is never in a conjunction with Venus while Vesta is retrograde due to Venus orbiting inside Earth's orbit and Vesta outside of it. A few recent and near-future Vesta–Venus conjunctions and squares that happen three times within about 5 months of each other follow:

2018: 1 square each in July, November, and December

2020: 1 conjunction each in April, May, and September

2021–2022: 1 conjunction in September 2021 and 2 in February 2022

MERCURY AND VESTA

The planet closest to the Sun represents the emergent mind within us in this life. Like Venus and Mars, the astrological element and modality are important to note, but integrating the elements, modalities, and signs with this planet is more important. Aside from the Ascendant (As), Descendant (Ds), Midheaven (Mc), and Home and Roots (Ic), Mercury, Venus, and the Moon and Sun have the most frequent conjunctions, squares, and oppositions with Vesta. The most important natal aspect (when compared with squares and oppositions) is a Vesta conjunction. When a person is born with Mercury and Vesta in conjunction, it means their archetypal sacred hearth is a potent contributor to their emergent mind, perception, communication, and thought processes.

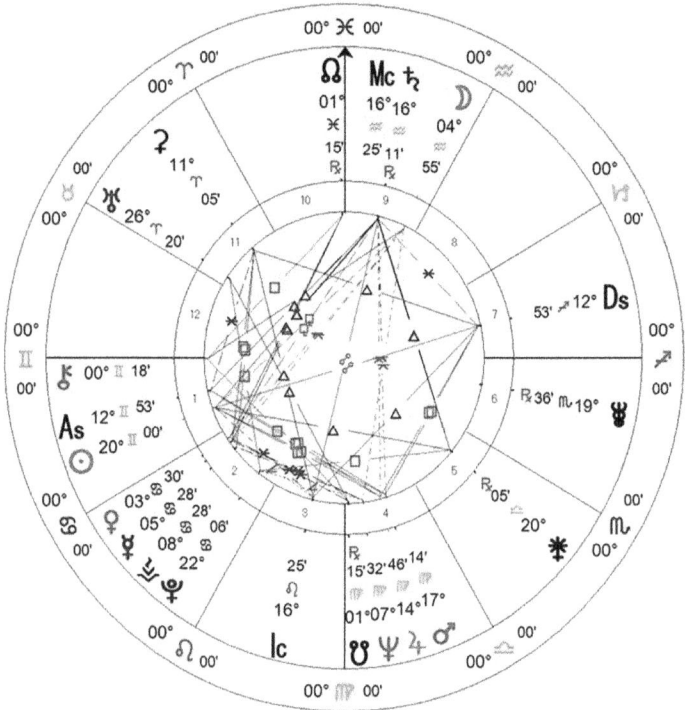

Fig. 4. Natal chart for Gene Wilder.

Gene Wilder
Male Chart
Jun 11 1933, Sun
3:50 am +6:00
Milwaukee, Wisconsin
43°N02'20" 087°W54'23"
Geocentric
Tropical
Whole Signs
True Node
Rating: AA

An example here is a client, Elaine, who I worked with for a few years. Elaine was born with Mercury and Vesta in conjunction in Leo and the eleventh house. When the Moon sign is different from the natal Mercury sign, then the differences between Mercury and the Moon become more evident. In this case, Elaine's Moon and Mercury are in different signs. The transmission of Leo in this combination becomes a highly vibrant, cerebral, and creative matrix concerned with learning about radical, radiant self-love (Leo) in a consciousness-expanding environment (eleventh house). Vesta imbues these qualities with a sacred layer inside her. Leo is an extroverted archetypal energy coming forth into the world that tunes into her sacred gift of a creative manifesting agent within. Her perceptions and viewpoint are intended to become larger, and dreaming big is a new narrative in this intuitive and fiery expression of Mercury. It taps into a combination of spontaneous creative impulses in the infinite arena of consciousness and celestial exploration.

Another example is actor, writer, comedian, and director Gene Wilder, known for his portrayal of Willy Wonka in the movie, *Willy Wonka and the Chocolate Factory*, among many other brilliant performances. He had an amazing ability to portray any role and shapeshift as required (Sun and Ascendant in Gemini; see Fig. 4). He was also born with an Aquarius Moon, something in shamanic astrology that could be called "coming from somewhere else or not originally from this world."

SUN AND VESTA

The Sun in shamanic astrology represents the archetypal "fuel" we burn to manifest our life purpose. It differs from other schools in Western astrology in that it is not the dominant force in our personality. The most important aspect between the Sun and Vesta in a natal chart is the conjunction, but opposition with the Sun is also important (for a different reason). A conjunction between Vesta with the Sun represents a direct line of deeper, archetypal insight that is more potent or charged in its expression. But the opposition between Vesta and the Sun highlights and expands the archetypal expression between the Sun's sign and the polarity with Vesta's sign.

The Sun, the center of our solar system, is also generally the center of the system's gravity well. From a geocentric perspective, the Sun "travels" in the sky along a specific path called the ecliptic or plane of the solar system. The ecliptic is where we find all of the planets in the sky to varying degrees.

Earth's tilt in relationship with the Sun determines seasonal patterns. This is the most important factor in understanding why the Sun is low at times in the south and high at other times and much higher in the sky, and in certain places at specific times on Earth, the Sun is directly overhead. The archetypes (signs) contain the essence of the seasons. Our modern calendar is based on the Sun being in a certain area of the sky in relation to Earth's equator. When a person is born with Vesta and the Sun in conjunction, it means your seasonal fuel's archetypal qualities are intended to be as sacred as the fire within the hearth of the home or the temple.

Vesta and the Sun have conjunctions, oppositions, and squares nearly every year with each other, and in the years when Vesta is in retrograde (which happens about every 16–17 months), there are three conjunctions or squares. In a person born at or near the time when Vesta is in opposition with the Sun, the Vesta archetype becomes more fully vibrant. Vesta is typically visible during the period within weeks of the Sun–Vesta opposition point and so it illuminates that person's Vesta sign. Vesta is then brought into focus, adding a deeper influence of that sign to the person's life.

Erik M. Roth

Moon and Vesta

Vesta and Earth's companion, the Moon, fall into a conjunction at least once a month and sometimes twice a month depending on Vesta's position in relationship to Earth. The Moon–Vesta conjunction is by far the most common of conjunctions, squares, and oppositions for Vesta, not including the chart angles (As, Ds, Mc, Ic). In my experience of giving readings over the years, I have found it more useful to focus on the nature of the Moon–Vesta conjunction rather than the squares or oppositions.

What does it mean to have a Moon–Vesta conjunction? In shamanic astrology, the Moon represents the catch-all of a person's lineage—family, ancestry, DNA, past-life themes, addictions, comfort zones, and archetypically speaking, what an individual mastered upon coming into this lifetime. Such conjunction means that Vesta plays a role in understanding one's overall lineage. Depending on the sign Vesta is in, it contributes a means of making a person's old story sacred. The gifts of the old story or lineage become reflected in a new light as well transmitted from the house that the Moon and Vesta are located in (if the same house).

Sir Elton John, the famed British musician, was born when Vesta and the Moon were in conjunction in Taurus (Fig. 5). Taurus is an archetype about receiving the sensuality, beauty, and bounty of the Earth. Considered the bon vivant of the signs, it relates to Aphrodite-like qualities. Elton's natal Moon and Vesta were in the tenth astrological house at the time of his birth and this creates a transmission/intent to use his lunar and Vesta archetypal qualities in a practical and constructive way.

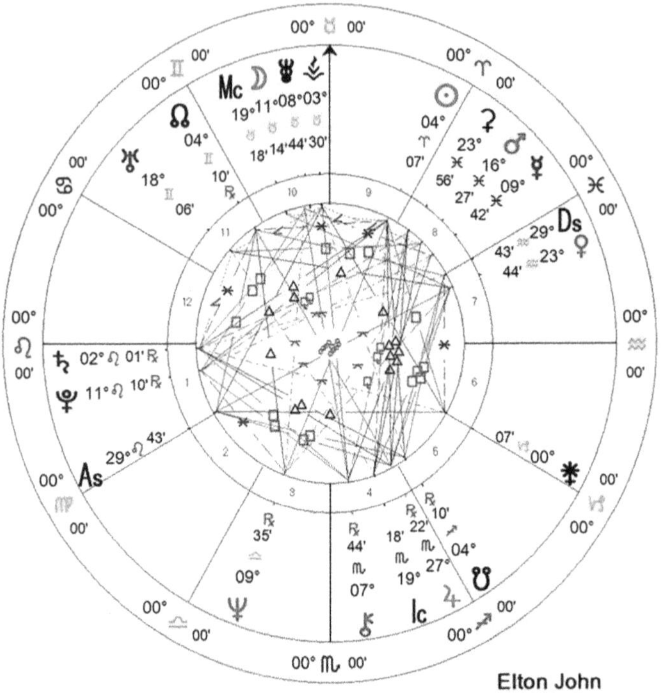

Fig. 5. Natal chart for Elton John.

Elton John
Male Chart
Mar 25 1947, Tue
4:00 pm BST −1:00
Pinner, England
51°N36' 000°W23'
Geocentric
Tropical
Whole Signs
True Node
Rating: A

Taurus is an earthy, physical, and creative archetypal energy—one can see how Elton John turned his love of the creative arts into something highly practical that blossomed into long-term results. Of course, in combination with Elton's natal Ascendant in Leo, it brought about a much greater public presence than would otherwise have occurred if his Ascendant was in Scorpio, for instance (as that would also have made his Moon–Vesta conjunction move to the seventh astrological house).

LUNAR NODES AND VESTA

The lunar nodes are intersection points in the orbit of the Moon around the Earth and the ecliptic (plane of the solar system) or crossroads between the Sun and Moon. In shamanic astrology, the North Node relates specifically to "future direction" or what loosely may be called "destiny." This node in a natal chart clarifies a person's archetypal life purpose as it relates to their Ascendant. The South Node helps clarify a person's archetypical past or lineage.

The lunar nodes move "backward" relative to the planets, Sun, and Moon across the sky. The nodes "move" or transit a *sign* completely about every 18 months; the nodes transit all of the signs every 19 years.

A person will experience the same Sun–Moon aspect (new moon, first-quarter, full moon, etc.) as it appeared when they were born every month, but it will only happen on the person's birthday every 19 years (meaning the same sign/degree in time). There is a near-halfway point at 9 years where this aspect is close on the person's birthday, but not as close or near-exact as the 19-year marker.

The most important feature of Vesta's relationship with the lunar nodes is the conjunction. Vesta and fast-moving planets (Mercury, Venus, and Mars) move into conjunction with a lunar node more frequently than the other planets. Vesta conjuncts twice with each node in a 5-year period, and thus for both nodes four times in 5 years.

A Vesta–South Node conjunction relates to lineage and especially past-life themes. This kind of conjunction would be similar to the Vesta–Moon conjunction.

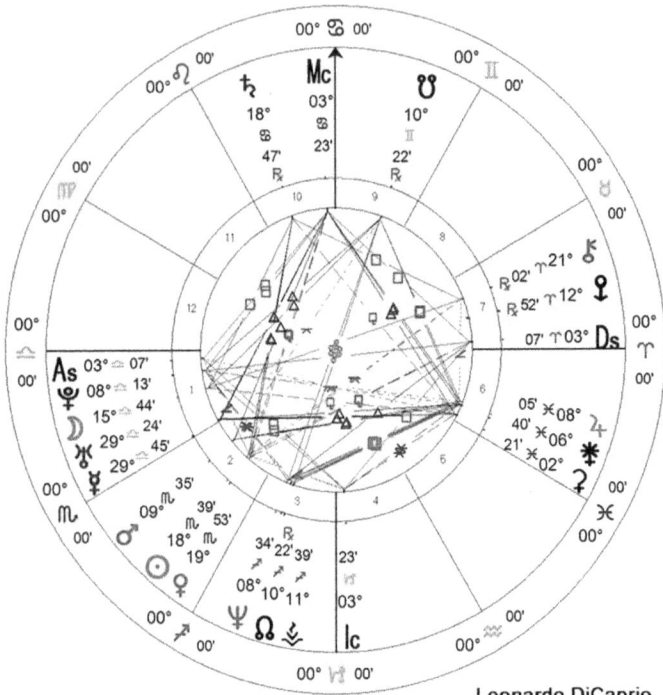

Fig. 6.

Natal chart for Leonardo DiCaprio.

Leonardo DiCaprio
Male Chart
Nov 11 1974, Mon
2:47 am PST +8:00
Los Angeles, California
34°N03'08" 118°W14'34"
Geocentric
Tropical
Whole Signs
True Node
Rating: AA

For people born with Vesta and the North Node in conjunction, Vesta is of vital importance to expression of life purpose. The word "sacred" can be injected into the description of their life purpose as it relates to the house of the north node and the Vesta archetype. It is also similar to having Vesta and Jupiter in the same sign and in conjunction with each other.

A great example of a person utilizing the gifts of a North Node–Vesta conjunction is well-known actor, producer, and activist Leonardo DiCaprio (see Fig. 6). The North Node and Vesta were only a degree apart at his birth in Sagittarius, a sign about exploring meaning, truth, and philosophy, with a knack for questing in life for those truths. Once found, those truths can become idealistic but also quite open to exploring deeper through causes, the sharing of the truth (no matter what it is) and making contributions to those truths. DiCaprio has taken on many documentaries as activist and actor to share information about climate change and animal welfare/rights.[25]

ANGLES AND VESTA

The most frequent of all conjunctions for Vesta (or any planet, really) occur with the angles of the natal chart. A chart angle refers to four points or two pairs, Ascendant–Descendant axis and the Midheaven–Home and roots axis. Every day, Vesta is in conjunction with all four angles, resulting in 1,460 conjunctions every year. The angles represent (along with Jupiter and the North Node) the most progressive parts of the natal chart, in that they change signs almost every two hours.

The Ascendant–Descendant axis is known as the "relationship axis," and the Midheaven (Mc)–Home and roots (Ic) axis as the "right livelihood axis."

Ascendant (As) = sign rising over the eastern horizon

Descendant (Ds) = sign setting on the western horizon

Midheaven (Mc) = sign at highest point of ecliptic in the sky

Home and roots (Ic) = sign opposite highest point of ecliptic

Each of the angles plays an important role in understanding one's life purpose. The Ascendant is the symbol for that which a person is a novice (archetypally)—their emerging

---

25   For details on his contributions during many years of activism, see https://en.wikipedia.org/wiki/Leonardo_DiCaprio.

identity. The Descendant is the sign that shows relationship intent (also part of the development of their inner beloved). The Midheaven shows archetypal qualities of one's vocation or calling in the world, and home and roots show the archetypal qualities to honor the home in 3D as well as the hearth within.

When Vesta is in conjunction with any one of these four angles, it adds the sacred qualities of that archetype to the angle. It comprises an extra layer of that archetype's importance in the person's life. If Vesta is conjunct an angle and in a different sign, then the latter adds an archetypal flavor to the person's Ascendant, Midheaven, or another angle on their chart.

For example, if a person was born with Vesta in conjunction with their Ascendant in the same sign, the Ascendant adds more of the sacred to the person's life. David Byrne, a musician and lead singer of the band Talking Heads, was born with an Ascendant–Vesta conjunction in the sign of Virgo (see Fig. 7). Virgo is a sign about understanding the patterning in various parts of life, highly detail-oriented, precise, analytical, and service through work. For David, this became evident in his music, both in his band and in his solo career with the weaving together of numerous dance and song styles/expressions. He also went on to do artwork and discuss the effects of architecture on music, with much of this relating to the emerging Virgo Ascendant and Vesta.[26]

---

26 See https://en.wikipedia.org/wiki/David_Byrne for details.

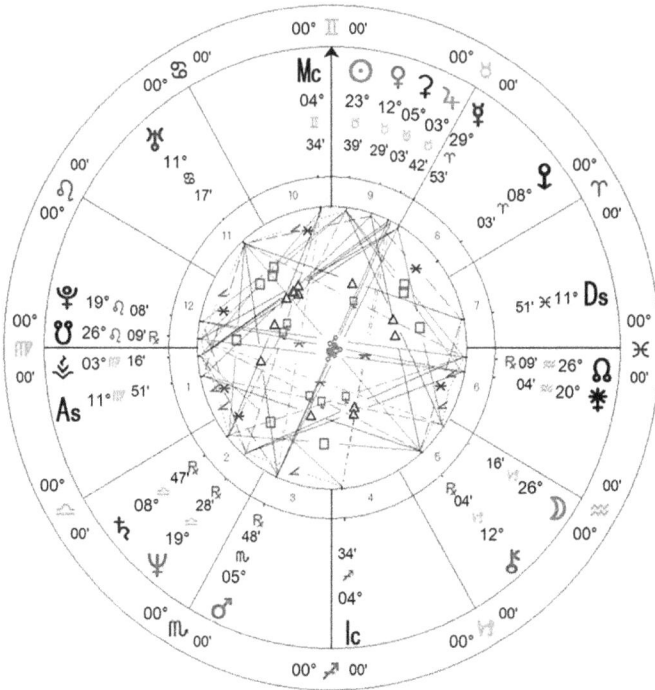

David Byrne
Natal Chart
May 14 1952, Wed
2:00 pm BST −1:00
Alexandria, Scotland
55°N59' 004°W36'
Geocentric
Tropical
Whole Signs
True Node
Rating: AA

Fig. 7. Natal chart for David Byrne.

Harnessing the Vesta Archetype

The archetype/sign that Vesta inhabits when we are born (combined with the house position) can provide a way to touch on the sacred in a way that shamanic astrologists have not previously experienced. The asteroid was aptly named not only in how it shows up for each of us, but also in its connection or sacred rhythm with the planet Saturn.

Connecting with Vesta, the asteroid (or planetoid), is the same as connecting with the ancient Vesta–Hestia mysteries. To utilize the benefits of the Vesta archetype/sign in one's life, it is best to begin with a basic level of understanding what the archetypes represent, and then reference the house position of Vesta's natal position. That particular archetype is made sacred, which means treating it as if it were something revered inside you, the immortal fire that burns as part of your soul's expression. The Vesta and Hestia temples contained the heartbeat of the community and the hearths the heartbeat of the home.

No archetype/house/planet is better than any other nor is it bad or good. The planetary bodies, Sun, and Moon are essentially indifferent to humanity's bad–good dualities. Vesta's mythological insights are also beyond duality, and this can assist us in gaining perspective in our own lives. Whatever the Vesta archetype in your life, it is a source for your gifts and soul rewards—in a way that contributes to what Jupiter and the Ascendant bring to our lives.

Vesta can also readily be incorporated in personal ceremony, especially during times when Vesta is activated in a planetary initiation (cycle). For example, if a person was experiencing a Saturn Return cycle (when Saturn returns to the same sign and degree of their natal Saturn position), then the archetypal qualities of Vesta become part of the Saturn Return.

It is a matter of feeling into the qualities within our Vesta archetype, determining where they can best be used. Ceremony itself is not limited to externals, such as an elaborate setup with candles, altars, priestesses, places of worship, reverence, or ancient sacred sites. The most basic form is simply to connect with yourself and your guides and/or Source meditation or prayer. Perfection in the tools you use is not necessary.

For example, the sacred expression of Vesta in Capricorn can be understood as the ability to create a strong foundation, to plant a seed for the long term. In fact, a real-world example is the conscious effort in organizing self to plant trees in one's own space or elsewhere or working with a group whose activism surrounding planting trees is felt to be more than symbolic. As the seedlings emerge from the soil and grow tall over time, they in turn share their knowledge with us in the form of their own fruits and seeds as well as creating harmonious and beautiful spaces in the world.

The potential meaning of Vesta in Gemini may be cultivating the imagination in creating a musical or play to entertain in a sacred way.

Temple de Vesta de Tivoli.JPG: LPLT -
Own work, CC BY-SA 4.0

Vesta in Pisces may manifest as making sacred the giving of love and spiritual blessings to an animal shelter for abused cats and dogs. There are countless ways to work with the archetypes in ceremony, harnessing them as we we become conscious of them in our lives. Ceremonies mark a special time period or event for a person or community or organization. Knowing one's natal Vesta archetype provides clues and insight as to how to experience Vesta in life. Ceremony can activate a person's Vesta archetype and allow it to "breathe" or be experienced in some fashion. From a Jungian psychological perspective, calling out one's archetype gives it life. Otherwise, the archetypal image sits in the unconscious creating complications that at times, unknown to the person, strongly influences their life. As Jung writes in *Four Archetypes*, "The archetype is essentially an unconscious content that is altered by becoming conscious and by being perceived, and it takes its colour from the individual consciousness in which it happens to appear."[27]

On rare occasions, Vesta becomes visible in the night sky at a particular point in its orbit relative to the Earth and Sun. These occasions occur only when the Sun is on the opposite side of the sky from Vesta (east or west), known as opposition (the most easily recognizable opposition is the full moon). During oppositions, Vesta is sometimes visible to the naked eye, and we can choose those days as ceremonial points or times for ourselves. Vesta could be visible for a few weeks leading up to the opposition and a few weeks after the opposition point. In astronomy, opposition is called "acronychal rise."

Like all other cosmological bodies, Vesta does not operate in a void—the rest of the solar system and humanity participate in its expression in countless ways. Inclusion of the other planets, chart angles, the Sun and Moon (and its nodes) are necessary to fully capture or realize the benefits that Vesta can bring into one's life.

---

27 C. G. Jung, *Four Archetypes: Mother, Rebirth, Spirit, Trickster*, trans. R.F.C. Hull, pbk. ed. (Princeton, NJ: Princeton University Press, 1970).

Reflections on the Large Asteroids and the Dwarf Planet Ceres

∽

Some astrologers incorporate the reading of asteroids in a given natal chart, especially the large ones: Ceres (reclassified in the twenty-first century as a dwarf planet), Vesta, Juno, Pallas Athena, and Hygeia. Another cometary body that is large enough to be incorporated in birth charts is Chiron, which orbits between Saturn and Uranus.

While Vesta is the only asteroid I have explored in detail, Ceres and Juno are also of great importance.

CERES

Ceres was the first asteroid to be identified in 1801, and reclassified by scientists in 2006 as a dwarf planet. It has some interesting return cycles (meaning that Ceres returns very close to its original position in relation to the Sun in a natal chart) for a person aged 23, 46, and 69, but Ceres is not visible to the naked eye.

Like Pallas Athena, Ceres has a 4.6-year orbital period. Also, like Pallas Athena, Ceres has an "orbital resonance" with Jupiter at the 83-year mark from one conjunction (meaning they return back to the point from an original given point after 83 years). Ceres and Jupiter have another conjunction near the original degree 83 years later. However, the orbital resonance between Pallas and Jupiter is more precise in comparison with the relationship between Ceres and Jupiter.

I believe that these return cycles/transits provide a deeper, more intimate look as to how we experience Ceres or the Great Mother in our lives. See the "Ceres and Vesta" section for details on mythology of Ceres and its meaning in a natal chart.

An interesting discovery was the fact that Vesta, Ceres, and Pallas Athena all return to (near) their original positions in the natal chart at age 69. This return appears to be really important but more research is needed to discover its astrological meaning.

JUNO

This asteroid, the third discovered by astronomers in the 1800s, was named for the goddess of marriage, Juno, who was bonded/married to Zeus/Jupiter. In ancient Greece, Juno was called Hera, and according to Demetra George and Douglas Bloch, "he-era" means "the earth."[28] Hera was revered as the celestial light, the immortal queen whose prominence matched that of Zeus/Jupiter. Among the most important of Hera's multiple aspects were reproductive power and the sanctity of the bond (as in the duality of masculine and feminine, heaven and earth, day and night, and so on).

In my research, which primarily consists of readings for people—how their natal chart and transits relate to their lives—I've found that Juno presents another strand of valuable information on understanding relationships as a structure or a concept beyond what Mars, Venus, and the Descendant show. Juno contributes to a person's chart when this asteroid is featured in aspect to other personal points on the chart, such as the Moon, Sun, or Venus, as well as when it is involved in cycles/transits.

In addition, when an outer planet, such as Saturn, aspects Juno, it does not comprise a "first-tier" cycle, but does

---

28   Demetra George and Douglas Bloch, *Asteroid Goddesses* (San Diego: ACS Publications, 1986), 150.

contribute to the storyline and provide additional insight to the person's archetypal concept of relationship, especially in the romantic and/or intimate sense. This asteroid carries the Libra archetype in its desire for conscious, equal partnership.[29] However, this influence is heavily modified in how Juno expresses, depending on the sign/archetype the asteroid is in at the person's birth as the house position and any outer planetary aspects in the natal chart.

Juno, as an asteroid, has a more irregular orbit than the planets. It does return close to its original degree on a person's birthday at certain points as summarized below:

Orbital period: 4.37 years

Duration in a sign: about 2-½ months (except when retrograde)

Important dates/returns: birthdays at 9, 13, 22, 26, 35, 48, 61, 84, and 96

2 orbits of Juno around the Sun = 9 years (close)

3 orbits of Juno around the Sun = 13 years (close)

5 orbits of Juno around the Sun = 22 years (close)

PALLAS ATHENA

This asteroid, named after the goddess of two names combined, represents wisdom, intellect, and feminine sovereignty. Originally as Athene or Athena, she rarely participated in battles among the gods, but when she did, she knew no equal. After she adopted her sister Pallas, the Amazon warrior goddess, that name was added. The name combination represents

29 George and Bloch state that Juno "symbolizes the principle of relatedness. Through the vehicle of committed partnership, she strives to realize a perfected and balanced union with another" (ibid., 157).

incorporating Athena within the culture, the mythology, of the emerging patriarchal nations. For diverse accounts of how the goddess's name(s) came to be, see George and Bloch's *Asteroid Goddesses*, as well as works by Robert Graves and Ginette Paris.

One of the more notable Athena stories is Prometheus's connection to this goddess. After Prometheus helped Athena come into the world from Zeus, Athena taught him valuable skills and breathed life unto the newly forged humans. The story of Athena and Prometheus alludes to Athena supporting Prometheus's action in stealing fire from the gods after Zeus attempted to withhold it from humans.[30]

I believe this is symbolic of Athena's nature in terms of resonance with the Aquarius archetype's revolutionary qualities. In another story, Pallas Athena bests Poseidon in a contest to settle a dispute between the Athenians and the newly migrated Ionians. But because the gods feared the wrath of Poseidon, they granted victory to him over Athena. This was another story symbolic of the emerging patriarchal power. From then on, Athens "deprived the Athenian women of their citizenship" and the "right to give their surnames to their children."[31] This gutted victory for the goddess represented the loss of matrilineal traditions in the region.

---

30 As summarized in http://www.mythencyclopedia.com/Pa-Pr/
Prometheus.html: "When Zeus and the other Olympian gods rebelled against the Titans, Prometheus sided with the gods and thus won their favor. He held Zeus's aching head so that Hephaestus (Vulcan) could split it open and release the goddess Athena. To show her gratitude, Athena taught Prometheus astronomy, mathematics, architecture, navigation, metalworking, writing, and other useful skills. He later passed this knowledge on to humans.

Prometheus created humans by shaping lumps of clay into small figures resembling the gods. Athena admired these figures and breathed on them, giving them life. Zeus disliked the creatures, but he could not uncreate them. He did, however, confine them to the earth and denied them immortality. Prometheus felt sorry for humans, so he gave them fire and taught them various arts and skills.

31 George and Bloch, *Asteroid Goddesses*, 86.

Regarding Pallas's importance in the natal chart, I believe that valuable information remains to be gleaned, based on its size (as a planetary body, on par with Vesta) and details from *Asteroid Goddesses*. One of Ceres's unique relationships with Pallas Athena is the similarity of its orbital period of 4.6 years. Also, like Ceres, Pallas Athena has an "orbital resonance" with Jupiter in that at the 83-year mark from one conjunction, Pallas and Jupiter have another conjunction at nearly the same exact degree of a given sign. These events occur at 18 orbital revolutions around the Sun for Pallas and 7 for Jupiter.

Orbital period: 4.62 years

Duration in a sign: 2-½ to 3 months (except when retrograde)

Important dates: Returns very close to birthdays 23, 46, 69, and 83

HYGIEA

While this book was in progress (November 2019), a new story was published about how the asteroid Hygeia (root of "hygiene"), named for the Greek goddess of health and daughter of Asclepius, could be considered a dwarf planet in the near future.[32] Hygiea is symbolized by a rod entwined with one or sometimes two snakes. This points to Asclepius and the origins of modern medicine. It is worth noting that Asclepius's teacher was the centaur, Chiron. The meaning of this asteroid in astrology may point to one's health overall and that the archetype/sign it inhabits may show areas of the mind and body

---

32   For information on the discovery, see www.universetoday. com/143897/asteroid-hygiea-is-round-enough-that-it-could-qualify-as-a-dwarf-planet-the-smallest-in-the-solar-system/

that require attention. It may also be used as a confirmation or could supplement what is learned from Chiron's position on the natal chart.

Orbital period: 5.57 years.

Duration in sign: Due to its eccentricity, Hygiea can be in a sign anywhere from 3 months to 10 months (varying due to retrograde period, nearing, and after opposition with the Sun). The mean is 5 to 6 months.

Important dates: About every 14 to 15 months, Hygiea is in opposition with the Sun. Synodic returns take place close to the original position of Hygiea on the natal chart at the 39th birthday. Other returns that are not as close take place at ages 11, 50, 78, and 89. For people born with Hygiea near the time it begins retrograde or during retrograde, the synodic return will not be as close.

Bibliography

∼

Bolen, Jean Shinoda. *Goddesses in Everywoman: Powerful Archetypes in Women's Lives*. New York: HarperCollins Publishers, 2014.

Downing, Christine. *The Goddess: Mythological Images of the Feminine*. New York: Crossroad Publishing Company, 1984.

Dumézil, Georges. *Archaic Roman Religion: With an Appendix on the Religion of the Etruscans*. Translated by Philip Krapp. Vols. 1 and 2. Baltimore: Johns Hopkins University Press, 1996.

George, Demetra, and Douglas Bloch. 1986. *Asteroid Goddesses*. San Diego: ACS Publications, Inc.

Giamario, Daniel, with Cayelin Castell. 2018. *The Shamanic Astrology Handbook*, revised and expanded 4th ed. Beaverton, OR: Shamanic Astrology Mystery School, Inc.

Goodwin, Erik D. 2012. *The Neurobiology of the Gods: How Brain Physiology Shapes the Recurrent Imagery of Myth and Dreams*. East Sussex, UK: Routledge.

Graves, Robert. 1960. *The Greek Myths*. Vols. 1 and 2, revised ed., reprinted in 1973. Baltimore: Penguin Books Ltd.

Graves, Robert. 1948 (1986). *The White Goddess*, amended and enlarged ed., 18th printing. Toronto: McGraw-Hill Ryerson Ltd.; New York: Farrar, Straus and Giroux.

De Santillanam, Giorgio, and Hertha von Dechend. (1969) 1977. *Hamlet's Mill: An Essay Investigating the Origins of Human Knowledge and Its Transmission Through Myth*. David R. Godine.

Hillman, James. 2007. *Mythic Figures: Uniform Edition of the Writings of James Hillman*, vol. 6.1. Putnam, CT: Spring Publications.

Jung, Carl. *Four Archetypes: Mother, Rebirth, Spirit, Trickster*. Trans. by R.F.C. Hull, pbk. ed. Princeton, NJ: Princeton University Press, 1970.

Murdock, Maureen. 1990. *The Heroine's Journey: Woman's Quest for Wholeness*. Boston: Shambhala Publications, 1990.

Pottenger, Rique, Neil F. Michelsen, and Zipporah Dobyns. 2008. *The Asteroid Ephemeris, 1900 to 2050: Ceres, Pallas, Juno, Vesta, Chiron and the Black Moon Lilith*. Exeter, NH: Starcrafts Publications.

Paris, Ginette. 1986. *Pagan Meditations: The Worlds of Aphrodite, Artemis, and Hestia*. Putnam, CT: Spring Publications.

Powell, Robert A. 2007. *History of the Zodiac*. San Rafael, CA: Sophia Academic Press.

Seltzer, Henry. 2015. *The Tenth Planet: Revelations from the Astrological Eris*. Bournemouth, England: The Wessex Astrologer Ltd.

Astrology/Astronomy Software Used by Author

Solar Fire Gold, v. 9.0.27, 2017. Sold by Astrolabe, programmed by Esoteric Technologies, Inc.

TimePassages™, adv. ed., v. 6.0.8, 2012. Astrograph Software, programmed by Henry Seltzer, Phoenix Toews.

Stellarium, v. 0.18.0, 2018. Free Software Foundation, Inc. Project coordinator and lead developer Fabien Chéreau. https://stellarium.org/

Appendix

❧

S ummarized here are the principal features of the Shamanic
Astrology Paradigm™ that originated from Daniel Giamario.
The text cited here derives from the Shamanic Astrology
Mystery School's public website (https://shamanicastrology.
com/faqs/the-shamanic-astrology-paradigm).

Shamanic Astrology: Essential Principles

The paradigm is informed by two underlying assumptions.

1. We do not incarnate into this life as a "blank slate," as ex-
    pressed in the idea that individuals are born without men-
    tal content, and therefore all knowledge comes from one's
    life experience or perceptions.

    The Shamanic Astrology Paradigm™ understands that at-
    titudes, habits, addictions, and expectations exist prior to
    encounters with our parents or the culture or historical
    time period in which we are raised. In other words, there
    is a (personal) nature *before* we experience nurture.

    This nature includes DNA, family history, possible past-life
    material, and a mysterious "other" component that includes
    a karmic package separate from DNA or family, similar to
    what author James Hillman described as the "acorn" when
    referring to the mysterious *daemon*, or inner awareness of
    divine powers guiding a person's life.

2. Our life has meaning and purpose that include an "original
    intent" directing us toward our life purpose. The Shamanic
    Astrology Paradigm™ is therefore more like Jungian psy-
    chology in that the bottom line is the quest for meaning
    and purpose, rather than the pursuit of sex, will, power,
    or even survival. Even if a higher meaning or purpose or

some transcendent, implicate order did not exist, our essence as a human being nevertheless is to create meaning and purpose.

Shamanic Astrology Paradigm™ Philosophical Framework

1. The priority in applying shamanic astrology is to describe the intended soul's journey. Because this intent can never be quantified, the Shamanic Astrology Paradigm cannot be proven by the use of statistics or deterministic scientific methodology.

2. Within the paradigm, there are no dualistic or hierarchical judgments of good---bad, higher---lower, or right---wrong. Further, this system perceives the doctrine of "rulerships" (including astrological concepts such as detriments and exaltations) as a relic of the past that traps an individual in historical relativity. The evolution of the paradigm includes continuous effort aimed at eliminating all manner of hierarchical language.

3. The paradigm is not a system of prediction, but rather an inquiry into original intent that leads us to consciously align with our personal intent (as revealed in the individual chart) as well as with universal intent (in co-creation with the Great Mystery).

4. The paradigm recognizes that objective time does *not* exist; therefore it is ultimately *not* possible for even the most gifted astrologer or the best astrological system to completely know or predict what will actually happen. This is because the astrologer is also a part of the greater unfolding of the *one reality* (Great Mystery), and therefore can never be truly objective to it or outside of it. It is, of course, possible to get close to this knowing and this is a good part of the thrill and value of astrology.

Shamanic Astrology Paradigm™ Foundational Elements

1. A unique understanding of the natal Moon. In this paradigm, the Moon position represents one's lineage, or who we were before our encounter with parents, culture, or the historical time frame when we incarnated. In shamanic astrology the view of the Moon has no connection to gender, including masculine and feminine elements.

    The Moon most clearly indicates the Mystery School we have previously mastered or have most closely identified with in the past. (The only other astrological school that had a similar, but by no means identical, view in seeing the Moon as the past was *esoteric astrology*. However, adherents to this school also considered the Moon as something dead or spent, with no relevance to the current life.)

    In this paradigm, the Moon is our lineage and comprises our attitudes, addictions, expectations, and an innate skill set. The Moon is our instinctive foundation, but can be a hindrance when we over-identify with it. Instead, our Moon is meant to be used in support of the current life purpose.

    (More recently, other astrologers began sharing this view. Much of mainstream astrology nevertheless maintains a rather patriarchal view of the Moon as exclusively female or mainly connected to feelings and emotions.)

2. A unique approach to the Ascendant, as well as the other chart angles. In the 1970s, much of mainstream astrology interpreted the Ascendant as physical appearance, how a person presented himself or herself to the world, and personality features or the persona. The Shamanic Astrology Paradigm™ sees it quite differently.

    The Ascendant clearly indicates the primary Mystery School being explored in the current life. The directional flow of the soul's journey is toward the Ascendant and it is almost always something quite new to the individual. Esoteric astrology also sees it this way.

It's interesting to note that in the original formulation of horoscopic astrology, the word "horoscope" meant the Ascendant and did not refer to the rest of the chart. The Shamanic Astrology Paradigm™ has a specific way of viewing the other three angles on the chart as also being entirely about current life intent.

3. The use of the Lunar Nodes by house position creating 144 storylines. The 144 storylines of lineage are determined by the South Node House with the sign of the Moon, and the 144 storylines of current life intent are determined by the North Node House with the sign of the Ascendant. The 12 house placements create 12 different versions of each of the 12 signs.

   The resulting 144 possible storylines are nuanced expressions of the basic archetypal patterns of life, that are revealed through the interweaving of the core meanings of the Moon, Ascendant, Lunar Nodes, and Houses. In this paradigm, whether referring to the lineage or the current life intent, these storylines are referred to as *the 12 jobs in the 12 tribes*, or *the 12 majors in the 12 Mystery Schools*.

4. Since 1999 the Shamanic Astrology Paradigm™ has used the whole sign house system exclusively. This is an ancient house system that simplifies the houses and eliminates confusion in several areas of chart interpretation. A discussion about this preference can be found in *The Shamanic Astrology Handbook*.

5. In the Shamanic Astrology Paradigm™ there is no special emphasis placed on Sun signs. The over-emphasis on Sun sign typecasting is viewed as a remnant of patriarchal and monotheistic consciousness and is therefore limiting and

outdated. Instead, the Shamanic Astrology Paradigm™ views the Sun as the symbol for the manifest expression of the Great Mystery itself. The Sun therefore, does *not* have any archetype projected onto it, including soul, self, or ego. Rather, the Sun is the energy or fuel that the seasons of the Earth's cycles contain and express.

6. The dynamic and evolutionary flow of the soul's journey is described using the technique of viewing the chart as three movements in a symphony, or three acts in a play, or a dialectic of thesis-antithesis-synthesis. This view reinforces the priority of intent, as opposed to a rigid and static description of personality. Further, this approach describes the soul's journey as a developmental process symbolized by the birth chart.

7. A unique approach to the use of Venus and Mars. Rather than the popular over-emphasis on the Sun sign, the Shamanic Astrology Paradigm™ perceives the sign of Mars on a man's chart to be the archetype of current life intent for a man. Similarly, the sign of the Venus position on a woman's chart indicates the archetype of current life intent for a woman. Therefore, the 24 different and specific expressions of masculinity and femininity hold considerably more archetypal significance than the Sun sign.

8. The inner sacred marriage process. In this paradigm, the sign of natal Mars for a woman initially indicates a projected longing, or the archetype of relationship that she will tend to look for outside herself. A man's Venus position similarly indicates his initially projected archetype and longing for wholeness. Whether successful or not in literally manifesting this projection, these archetypes offer a significant clue for what needs to develop internally in order to arrive at inner wholeness. The Shamanic Astrology Paradigm™ therefore posits that the path of relationship can

become an addition to one's wholeness, rather than maintaining that a partner is necessary in order for a person to feel complete.

9. The six paths of relationship/partnership. The paradigm uses an innovative approach for discovering the current life intent for partnership and relationship. These six paths are derived from the pairing of the Ascendant/Descendant and are often very different than what the culture has believed is the path to relationship.

10. Transit cycles are perceived as indicating the varieties of initiation. This paradigm divides the cycles of initiations into three worlds or realms of experience.

- Upper world (celestial world), using Neptune and Uranus
- Middle world (the ordinary, apparently linear world of objective reality that occurs in real time) using Saturn, Jupiter, and the Lunar Nodes
- Lower world (or underworld), using Pluto and Chiron

During the course of a lifetime, these cycles of initiation do *not* flow in a linear fashion. Any type of cycle could conceivably follow any other type of cycle. Most importantly, as with all other aspects of the paradigm, the various initiatory processes are never perceived as being either "good" or "bad," but rather what is needed to achieve the intent of the initiation cycle.

11. The shamanic timeline. In addition to the cycles of initiation as indicated by the transits of the outer planets, the Shamanic Astrology Paradigm™ uses a unique approach to the planetary cycles as measured from their positions at birth, such as the Saturn return, the Jupiter return, and so on. Using this technique, it is possible to know which initiatory processes a person is undergoing simply by knowing their age.

12. The use of synodic cycles of Venus, Mars, and Mercury. The Shamanic Astrology Paradigm™ pioneered the reintroduction of the use of synodic cycles into modern astrology. The knowledge of the phases of these cycles helps to place an individual chart into the context of a much larger story. In addition, the synodic planetary return cycles are a crucial ingredient of the Shamanic Timeline.

13. Knowledge of the turning of the ages. The paradigm introduced the phrase "the turning of the ages" in the 1980s. This knowledge and direct experience of the intersection of the zodiac and the plane of our galaxy with the solstices and equinoxes over time provide a larger context for understanding the importance of our current era including the end and beginning of a 26,000-year cycle. From this foundation we have the basis for understanding how the astrological signs and symbols, as well as the human and mythic storylines, change over time.

14. The paradigm integrates the sign (seasonal zodiac) with the sidereal zodiacs (the 12-fold divisions of the sky or constellations). The logo for the Shamanic Astrology Mystery School beautifully illustrates this integration (see cover of *The Shamanic Astrology Handbook*).

15. The Shamanic Astrology Paradigm™ stems from the unique chart analysis techniques combined with continual connection and direct experience with the night sky, including regular, kinesthetic experiences of the seasons, the cycles of the Sun, Moon, and visible planets, along with the constellational patterns. The insights of the Shamanic Astrology Paradigm are derived primarily from this personal, direct relationship, equally valuing astrology and astronomy. In fact, the full certification track for an initiated shamanic astrologer requires the night sky component. The aim of

this paradigm is for practitioners to form a personal relationship with the planetary and stellar patterns.

16. The Shamanic Astrology Paradigm™ has a "naked eye" emphasis. Shamanic astrology is designed to be functional at any time in history, with or without the aid of technology or telescopic enhancements.

17. The Shamanic Astrology Paradigm™ recognizes as its foundation the Hermetic dictum, "As Above, So Below, As Within, So Without." Within this paradigm, the dictum is not merely an intellectual philosophy but an actual reality, requiring the knowledge and experience of the seasons and cycles of the Earth in space. This reality is part of a perennial, magical worldview, and is not the same as the scientific, cause-and-effect, and more deterministic "modern" worldview.

About the Author

Based in Oregon, Erik Roth has been reading charts since 2010. He is a fully initiated and certified shamanic astrologer as trained by Daniel Giamario and the Shamanic Astrology Mystery School. Erik has shared the powerful tool of shamanic astrology with thousands of people on the West Coast through lectures, holistic and psychic fairs, and classes taught in-person and online. See inspiralnexus.com for his YouTube and podcast recordings, as well as his newsletter.

Erik is also managing director of the Shamanic Astrology Mystery School, where he provides administrative, logistical, and website support, as well as playing a support role in co-facilitating webinars and teleclasses centered on Giamario's Shamanic Astrology Paradigm™.

Erik continues to learn and expand his knowledge of astrology through skywatching, the readings he gives, and the classes he teaches, along with teachings and insights from other astrologers, mythologists, and psychologists.

For more information about the Shamanic Astrology Mystery School, please visit: www.shamanicastrology.com

www.ingramcontent.com/pod-product-compliance
Lightning Source LLC
La Vergne TN
LVHW011210080426
835508LV00007B/709